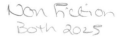

Non Fiction
Both 2025

CW00816368

WE DID WHA

Matador
9 Priory Business Park,
Wistow Road, Kibworth Beauchamp,
Leicestershire. LE8 0RX
Tel: 0116 279 2299
Email: books@troubador.co.uk
Web: www.troubador.co.uk/matador
Twitter: @matadorbooks

ISBN 978 1788037 976

British Library Cataloguing in Publication Data.
A catalogue record for this book is available from the British Library.

Typeset in 11pt Cambria by Troubador Publishing Ltd, Leicester, UK

Matador is an imprint of Troubador Publishing Ltd

WE DID WHAT WE HAD TO

John Hill and Pamela Howarth

In memory of Courtney Gilliatt, DFC., my WWII Canadian pilot, who remained a close friend until his death in 2008.

Also in memory of Iain Purves, Past President of the Canadian Chapter of the RAF regiment, whom I met during my first return trip to Canada in 2002. A good friend and important link with all my connexions in that country.

Per ardua ad astra

About Pamela Howarth

Pamela hails from Warwickshire and now lives in a Rutland village, with her partner and their dog, Sheba. She has three adult sons and a small grandson.

In her working life, she taught English for many years at secondary level, then specialised in dyslexia tuition and was a study adviser at the universities of Lincoln, Leicester and the OU. Now retired from teaching, she has discovered writing, having recently published a biography of Shakespeare, *Befriend the Bard!* She jokes about suffering from late-onset writing compulsion.

She describes helping her uncle with *We Did What We Had To*, as one of the most worthwhile things she has done. "I'm very proud of my uncle and have so enjoyed helping him to write this book. His story should be told... lest we forget".

She would very much like to help others tell their life stories. Find out more about her books and writing services from her website: www.pamelahowarth.com

Table of Contents

How this book came about

Johnny Hill, full name John Henry Charles Hill, is my uncle and he's currently busy planning his 95th birthday party for next January. I've known him all my life and have fond childhood memories of the part he played in family gatherings in London and the Midlands, not to mention holidays we all spent together in Cornwall.

In common with many families, we've seen less of each other as we children have grown up and gone our separate ways. The usual generational diaspora. Then, there are always deaths. Uncle J., as I call him, was married to my dad's sister, Betty, who died in 2004, my father, Richard, (Dick) having died in 1980. As happens, we only seemed to meet up at weddings and funerals, so recently we have been determined to get together more regularly. First there was my uncle's 90th birthday party, and then there was another reunion, thankfully before my mum became ill and died. Her death, in January 2015, has brought me to the kind of refocussing which can occur at various key stages of life. I've written a short memoir for my three sons to give them some sense of their family history, and this year I decided that I wanted to ask my uncle about his wartime experiences in the RAF, if he was willing to talk about them... He was.

* * *

I'll take you back – briefly – to the late 1950s/early 1960s. The place Padstow, now rather famous for its associations with the poet, John Betjeman, and more recently for Rick Stein's fish restaurants. In summer, and sometimes at Easter, too, we used to rent the larger half of a huge bungalow up on the hillside overlooking the sea. There were eight of us: my parents, my younger brother, Anthony and I, plus the Hill family: Johnny and Betty, with their two daughters, Wendy and Catherine, who were the same ages as my brother and I, born in 1948 and 1952. Our grandparents sometimes came too, making the numbers up to ten. They loved Cornwall and had in younger days spent many happy holidays on the opposite coast at Looe. Both seemed very elderly to me, though they were probably not a lot older than I am now.

Most days the sun shone, or so it seemed. If it didn't, we children had an attic room up a wooden ladder where we slept and played. The perfect den, away from the grown-ups. Very Enid Blyton. We were the *Famous Four*. A lot of the time we all headed into Padstow, walked around the quaint harbour and up the steepish hill the other side. The path led round the cliffs where there was any number of sandy bays, perfect for swimming, picnicking, rock-climbing, etc. We colonised favourite spots on the rocks, spreading tartan rugs and all our beach paraphernalia. My dad and my uncle were always unofficially in charge of organising games... they were both extremely good at it. Whether it was French cricket, rounders, piggy-in-the-middle, races to the sea, sandcastle competitions... it was always fun. And probably vital to warm us up if we'd just been for a dip in the sea, which was usually freezing. Though there were a lot of rock-pools which were warmer and where you could spend hours looking for sea creatures and shells. Some, especially at Treyarnon, were deep enough to bathe in and ideal for children. My dad spent hours when I was eight, teaching me to swim in one of them, holding me less and less, so the magic moment came when I realised he'd let go and that I was doing it on my own.

If they sound innocent days, that's because they were! We had no idea that we were living only 10 or 15 years after the finish of WW2 and that we wouldn't exist if any of our parents had been killed in the six years that it took over their lives.

Don't Mention the War!

As a child, growing up in a pleasant suburban house in Leicester, I wasn't aware of any of the stuff they'd been through. It didn't seem to be talked about. Even in adult conversations which I was rather good at listening in to. (I was that kind of child.) As I got older, and affluence in the country grew and there were far more things to buy in the shops, including new kinds of food, I became more aware of the fact that my country had recently fought in a war and won. That some parts of the country still had heaps of rubble and bomb-damaged buildings. That there hadn't been much food, let alone sweets and chocolate. My mother, for example, was still very careful with eggs and treated them as special, not to be used extravagantly. At school, both primary and secondary, I was in large classes – a *bulge year* it was called, again something to do with the war, though I didn't understand what. There were quite a few war films being made and stories appeared in my brother's comics. (Not mine: across the gender-divide, I took *The Girl*.) The enemy apparently had been the Germans, usually called the *Hun*. Later, in our teens, my brother was to take his German penfriend to the cinema, not realising that they were showing a war film. Embarrassing moment.

A few men still went around calling themselves *Major* or *Captain* or *Wing Commander,* when they weren't in the forces anymore; presumably because they'd had what my parents called a *good war*, whatever that meant. How could you have a good war, I wondered. War was bad, wasn't it? Though it made for exciting stories in the way that cowboys and Indians did. Looking back on my childhood, I think most adults probably shared a huge sense of relief, an embracing of order and everyday routine and a heartfelt gratitude that things were getting better all the time. Most were ready and able to move on, as we say today. Though, of course, as I know now, some would never be able to.

Johnny Hill, though, had had a good war.

As I grew older I learnt that my father had been in a reserved occupation (tax inspector) and that Uncle Johnny

WE DID WHAT WE HAD TO

had been in the RAF. When I went to visit my cousins in Harrow, there was a wedding photo on the piano of him looking very smart in his uniform; my aunt wore a very elegant bias-cut dress and carried an enormous bouquet.

Family banter included semi-humorous references to my uncle's skill at planning routes and map-reading if we were going on a trip out somewhere. Even today he makes wry jokes about how he *should* be able to get from A to B without a problem... I didn't get the joke for ages, even when I discovered he'd been a navigator in the war, as I didn't know what a navigator was. Just another example of impenetrable adult humour.

It wasn't until I was much older, studying, then teaching literature, that I read around writers' backgrounds and improved my knowledge of history, including the two 20th-century world wars. (I still have some yawning gaps, though.) Later, my own children were studying WW2 in History, which seemed very modern compared with my own school syllabus which leapt crazily from the Romans to the Tudors and Stuarts to the French Revolution, with nothing in between or after, it seemed. Two of my sons went on 'A' level History trips to Berlin, which included a visit to Sachsenhausen concentration camp (which they found very moving), as well as lots of unofficial trips to German beer cellars to let off steam afterwards.

I'm history now, jokes my uncle, as his great grandchildren borrow his RAF log-book for projects at school.

Time I talked to him about what he actually *did* in the war. Time I found out about his RAF service at first hand.

Time I asked him what planes he'd actually flown in... His great-grandchildren knew more than me, for goodness sake!

* * *

So... I went down to Leigh-on-Sea, Essex, to stay with my uncle in the spring of this year for five days. And we talked. And talked. My cousin, Wendy, came too, sitting in on some sessions and supplying us with cups of tea and pieces of fruit cake. I recorded our conversations on my phone and transcribed them afterwards. It didn't actually take too long as my uncle had already organised the sessions and divided his subject matter neatly and chronologically into three sections. In the past, he'd given some talks about his war, so this had probably fed into his planning. He'd no doubt refreshed his memory about details, too, but the sharpness of his recollection was amazing. He spoke fluently, without reference to his notes, sometimes for two hours at a stretch. He recalled key names, dates and details, only hesitating occasionally to find an apt word or to include an afterthought. I had very little to do except respond and occasionally query something. The whole lucid narrative seemed to be fully formed in my uncle's head, experience remembered with clarity across the years.

It's interesting that the longest section was that relating to training, rather than to active service. Funny stories of all sorts peppered this first section, not always ones about young men being young men, though these featured, too. The training part was utterly fascinating, as it shed so much light, not only on the thoroughness of the whole process, but on the commitment of the young men undergoing it, as well as the response of others *to* them, the warmth of Brits, Canadians and Americans they met. Of course, the camaraderie of the war is well documented, as is the social and political background to the 1940s. What gave me pause for thought, having been born after the war, was the way ordinary lives were affected, literally overnight, and how all generations, but especially the young adults, had to put their normal dreams, plans and aspirations on hold for the unforeseeable future – which might not be a very long one. A whole new world – *you could say a brave, new world* – of values and expectations, is superimposed, including, of course, the reality of untimely death. The winding path to experience and maturity becomes a huge highway, where everything moves at speed.

* * *

The character of my uncle permeates his narrative, of course, and I'm not just talking about his strong sense of the ridiculous or his quick wit.

Clearly sociable and fun-loving, he is also thoughtful and serious-minded. I won't go on (much) as I don't want to embarrass him, but I do think that his strong moral sense and his equable temperament must have helped him to cope with the uncertainties of war and the dangers faced regularly during active service. He says that he doesn't think he felt nervous very often… Flying ops soon became a kind of job, a job he had to do to the best of his ability. Was his level-headedness partly innate, partly instilled through training?

Indirectly, throughout the narrative, his view of war is revealed, showing a humanity and an ability to see the wider picture. He and his botany-loving pilot were not crazed by the daring-do of flying and fighting, nor were their values skewed by the jingoism of war. Though, it was true, he said, that many of the navigators were British, as it was thought that they would act as a restraining influence on some of the more gung-ho Australian and Canadian pilots.

Which brings me to the section on active service. It was almost as if he didn't – still – want to talk much about this. A mix of modesty and of restraint in discussing something which, after all, involved an extreme way of resolving conflict, part of mankind's history since the time he started moving around and disputing territory. This war, more than almost any other, was an ideological one, which sought to put an end to an evil regime, but it was still war. My uncle, a practising Christian who still sings in his church choir, often used the following phrase in his account of the missions they flew: *We did what we had to do*. This says it all really; hence it has become the title of our book.

Some wartime accounts go deeper into the armaments and military machinery possessed by both sides. I think my uncle could talk the talk if he wanted but chose not to. He'd rather leave it out.

I subsequently asked him if he would elaborate a bit on the types of enemy fire encountered, as I'd come across descriptions in other accounts and was hazy about the terminology, for example, *flak* and *ack-ack* (anti-aircraft) guns. Apparently, flak (from the German *Fliegerabwehrkanone*, literally *flier/defence/gun*) can't be seen in daylight until it explodes, rather like a firework, but at night you can see a stream of light. Phrases like *Bandit astern!* to give warning of an enemy plane captured my imagination, but then I'm at a safe distance from ever needing to use it. I genuinely wanted to know what it had looked like up in the skies, what it sounded like, what it smelled like even. Other need-to-know details involved practicalities that my uncle would take for granted having been there, like where he sat, how he read his maps in the dark and so on. (The answer to the last question was with a torch, but even that had paper strips over the beam to keep it very low.) One thing he did tell me that has stayed in my mind is how he sometimes had to pull the joystick during the countdown – 700ft, 600ft, 500ft etc. – to get the plane out of a near-fatal dive when his pilot, Court, was focussed on attacking a target. So much concentration, energy and adrenalin is involved in attack mode, he explained, that the navigator has to keep a cool head and, on occasion, take over the essentials of flying, given the time lag before the plane responds. I think both of them in that Mosquito cockpit must have kept each other alive time and time again. Routinely.

* * *

And so the narrative evolved. I read around the subject with the help of some of my uncle's books on the Mosquito and some useful detail on the Internet, so I felt I understood better what he was telling me. I was struck by another phrase my uncle used: *By guess or by God.* No matter how thorough the training, I realised, nothing would prepare you for the actual hazardous conflict in the skies where you just followed your instinct at times. So much depended on human skill and human error, as well as on happenstance. On God. You only have to read the third and last part of Johnny's narrative to realise what terrible twists of fate, in this case training accidents, led to the ceremonies in that little graveyard in Canada.

As I wrote up the active service section, I also married up the meticulous recording in my uncle's log-book with my transcript. The log book is the most incredible, irrefutable and authentic piece of documentation in this whole story. Anyone who looks at is struck by the way it brings the war right into their living room; reading its spare prose brings a vivid mental picture of these two men flying the night skies over Europe, alone in that cramped cockpit in the dark.

My uncle needed the logbook back for another interview – this time with someone from the De Havilland Aircraft museum – so I made sure it went door to door with one of the reliable delivery companies. As my uncle says, relishing the irony, several buses always come along at once. The yellowed pages don't see the light of day for years and then his great-granddaughter gets given a school project and two interviewers arrive on the doorstep, one of them me. The museum interview saw the living room transformed into a film set, and, as I write, a documentary is being made involving several airmen who flew Mosquitoes in the war. Apparently, my uncle is the youngest, the oldest being ninety-nine.

During the time I was helping my uncle with his story, I met Dennis who lives in my village, Edith Weston, and is now in his eighties. We got talking and it turned out he'd been in the RAF, a member of ground-crew stationed at RAF North Luffenham, just after the war. We soon started talking about the famous twin-engine Mosquito fighter-bomber, clearly his favourite plane, and he came out with the following comment:

The Mosquitoes did all the work, but the Spitfires got the glory!

I asked him if I could quote him in this book and he agreed, whole-heartedly.

Another rendezvous, another family get-together, so valuable to all of us now, this time during a glorious autumn in Rutland, included a bit more talking and a bit more tweaking of the narrative, not to mention some amendments of details I'd got wrong.

This inspirational story cries out for illustration by the photos my uncle has kept, by documents and, of course, by the logbook, all of which have such poignancy today. Sometimes a picture *does* speak louder than words. There are many familiar secondary source pictures from archives – wartime newspaper cuttings, photos of planes and young men who flew in them… but these are of someone I know and all help to immortalise one young man's wartime experience, giving understanding to those fortunate enough not to have lived through it.

Above all, as a post-war child, I want to thank my uncle and all those who fought and all those who died for our island's freedom during World War II.

I hope this book will, in a small way, help to commemorate them.

Pamela Howarth
October 2016

Part 1

Pre-War Childhood and Education
1922–1939

I am the elder son of my parents, Charles and Ethel Hill, both of whom were Irish. My father was born in the village of Coolniddan, near Macroom, County Cork, and my mother was born in Kinsale, County Cork. They each had eleven siblings, my mother being the eldest of her family; and remarkably they both came from Protestant families.

I was born on the 21st January 1922, in Camberley, Surrey. I was a pupil at Yorktown Elementary School, from where, in 1933, I won a scholarship to Frimley and Camberley County Secondary school. I represented the latter school at both football and cricket, a high point being in 1936 when I was in the school football team which won the Surrey Grammar Schools Under-15 Cup, beating Kingston Grammar School in the final. During my time at Grammar School, I won both the annual

Junior and Senior Cross-country Runs, and when I left in 1939, I was the holder of the School one-mile record. Scholastically, I passed the Schools Certificate examination, with exemption from Matriculation, winning the History prize for the highest marks in this subject.

My brother and I were choirboys at St Paul's church, Camberley, in the Parish where the gentry and 'well-to-do' resided. As a result of this, we attended several 'mini' society weddings for which we received two shillings each time; very welcome money in those days.

I was also a member of the local Frimley and Camberley Cadet Corps, which was affiliated to the 5th Battalion Royal Queen's Regiment. Because of the large number of retired senior military personnel living in the area, we obviously had several benefactors with influence in the right places. Consequently, most of our instructors were Army ones employed at the nearby Royal Military College (RMC), Sandhurst. We received training in drill, rifle drill, PT, gymnastics and signalling. We were allowed to hold our annual Athletic meeting at the RMC running track, and to train there beforehand. We also enjoyed annual summer camps on the Isle of Wight for which the cost was minimal.

I had two very memorable experiences which came from my membership of the Cadet Corps. During the 1938 summer holidays, there was an organised one-week tour of the World War I battlefields in France. Four of us from my corps went, along with other UK cadets and school units. I remember that for us the cost was very much subsidised. We were housed in French Army Barracks in Soissons. The highlight of the trip was participating in a parade in Paris, marching along the Champs Elysees to the Arc de Triomphe for a very moving ceremony.

The second took place one Sunday morning, *(May 2nd 1937)* when King George V1 visited the Royal Military College. If my memory is correct, I think it was associated with the dedication of a new or renovated organ in the College Chapel. It was arranged that after the Church service the King would inspect our Cadet Corps. What an honour it was for me!

When, in 1939, I was accepted for employment in the Civil Service, I had to provide two character references, I was able to provide one from a retired brigadier, and the other from a retired admiral!

As I pen this, I realise what hard times they must have been for my parents. We lived in a council house on a council estate. Although my father had regular employment as a waiter at the RMC, he was not paid very much. But to ensure that my brother and I were well looked after, both our parents worked every spare hour they had. My father had afternoons off as he was required to work evenings, so, in addition to tending his own garden and allotment, he did gardening for the gentry. He also worked as a caddy at the local golf course. My mother did domestic cleaning work and took in laundry. For a time she worked for the author, Daphne du Maurier.

We had a very happy childhood for which I cannot thank my parents enough.

I left school at the beginning of 1939, having passed the Civil Service Clerical Officer open examination and, on 6th March 1939, joined the Air Ministry, working in the Equipment Directorate in Berkeley Square House, Berkeley Square.

Part 2

The Eve of War to the End of RAF Training 1939–1944

Significant events of WW2
1939

- 1st September: Germany invades Poland.
- 3rd September: Britain, Australia, New Zealand and France declare war on Germany.
- 4th September: RAF attacks German Navy.
- 5th September: The USA proclaims its neutrality.
- 10th September: Canada declares war on Germany.
- The Battle of the Atlantic begins but in Europe there is a period of limited activity known as the *Phoney War*.

The United Kingdom: September 1939–June 1943

In the infamous year of 1939, I was a raw 17-year-old.

I'd started work in March as a clerical officer at the Air Ministry, a branch of the Civil Service, grandly located in Berkeley Square, London, where a nightingale sang, according to the famous song. I commuted into the West End from Camberley, Surrey, where I lived with my parents. My younger brother, Peter, had already left home in 1938, aged 15, and joined the RAF as a boy entrant. At the Air Ministry, I worked for the Directorate of Equipment, my particular section being responsible for barrack stores, i.e. plates, cups and saucers and so on.

As the year wore on, it became pretty obvious that things were hotting up in Europe and by late summer we had to work overtime in the evenings. I remember leaving around 8ish, one lovely summer's evening, and seeing lots of taxis drawing up outside the Mayfair Hotel, disgorging men in tuxedos and ladies in long dresses for a dinner dance with *Ambrose and his Orchestra*. As the saying goes, *the band played on*.

Then, a few days before the outbreak of war, an edict came round to the effect that all staff who were over an hour's journey from home had to sleep in the office, the idea being that if war was declared and the Germans immediately bombed London, then government departments would have to be evacuated at a moment's notice. I was one of those who had to camp out in the office.

I remember that on Saturday 2nd September, I went to see Arsenal, the football team I supported, play Sunderland at Highbury. The weather was hot and sunny, and Arsenal won! The score – 5:2 – is etched on my memory. I can still remember the names of the entire team, but suffice to say that Ted Drake, the Centre Forward, scored four of the five goals.

On the next day, 3rd September, as everyone knows, the Second World War started.

By the Monday morning, our evacuation had started. We were being sent we knew not where, to the mysterious Department. ZA. The plan was for one representative from each section of the Air Ministry to be sent first as a kind of advance party. All my colleagues, many of whom were married and no doubt wanted to get home to see wives and children, volunteered me to go first, on the plausible grounds that I was young, single and already had my overnight bag at the office!

I couldn't dispute this, so at midday, with no time to let my parents know, I was collected in the clothes I stood up in, by one of three Daimler cars, and driven north out of the capital for the unknown destination of Department ZA. Several hours later, we drew up at the Grand Hotel in Harrogate, Yorkshire, one of many hotels which the government had requisitioned, and certainly the finest I had ever set foot in. I'm not sure to this day of the need for the advance party as we had nothing to do for days, except to find permanent digs, which I duly did. I was to stay at my comfortable billet, a former guesthouse, belonging to Hetty and her husband, Dan, for three happy years, until I joined the RAF in 1942. The postal service in those days was so good (three deliveries a day) that I could soon let my parents know where I was and get my clothes and belongings sent on to me. I could even send washing home and be sure of getting it back by the end of the week, often with a cake included in the parcel. With a bit of initiative, I did a deal with a local Chinese laundry to get my five detachable shirt collars washed for three shillings a week.

I was a free agent for the first time in my life! From the social point of view, I soon got to know all sorts of colleagues, with whom I'd previously only been on surname terms, such was the formality of the Civil Service and many workplaces in those times.

Harrogate had numerous pubs, five cinemas, an opera house for all manner of different shows (with Trevor Howard, Rosalind John and others) and the Royal Hall for concerts and dances. The Air Ministry also organised a good deal of entertainment and took over the playing fields of Ashville College, a local private school, for football, tennis and cricket. As I loved sport, this was an added bonus. So was the government decision to extend daylight hours by putting the clocks forward two hours. It didn't get dark till about 11pm, which meant I could play for the local cricket club until late into the evening, though cow pats in their outfield meant you didn't attempt any fancy fielding.

Life was good! We may not have had much money but you could make an extra three shillings by volunteering for fire-watching. There were six of us in my digs, and we all paid our landlady the going rate of one guinea a week for board and lodging, including breakfast and evening meals, so inevitably all the evacuees across town became known as *guinea pigs*. In addition, the six of us did a deal with our landlady, paying her 10 shillings a week each for a cooked lunch as well. We had large appetites in those days, and the food was good, though rationing had begun in 1940. Hetty's nephew had useful connections with a local butcher, and husband, Dan, had an allotment *(Dig for Britain)*, so we ate very well, compared to some people in different parts of the country.

For a shilling you could have a jolly good evening out: 6 pence for a seat in the *gods* (the Upper Circle) at the theatre, 2 pence for a programme and 4 pence for fish and chips on the way home.

Significant events of WW2
1940

- 16th March: Germany bombs Scapa Flow naval base, Scotland.
- 9th April: Germany invades Norway and Denmark.
- 10th May: Nazis invade France, Belgium, the Netherlands and Luxembourg.
- 10th May: Winston Churchill becomes Prime Minister.
- 15th May: Holland surrenders.
- 28th May: Belgium surrenders.
- 3rd June: British Expeditionary Force is evacuated from Dunkirk (Operation Dynamo).
- 10th June: Italy declares war on Britain and France/ Norway surrenders.
- 22nd June: France signs an armistice with Germany and Hitler tours Paris.
- 1st July: German U-boats attack British merchant ships in the Atlantic.
- 10th July: The Battle of Britain begins.

WE DID WHAT WE HAD TO

- 23rd August: first air raids on London begin.
- 25th August: British air raid on Berlin.
- September 1940: German invasion of Britain (Operation Sea Lion) is planned, but later postponed until 1941.
- 7th September: *Blitzkrieg* begins on London and major cities.
- 13th September: Italy invades Egypt.
- 15th September: victory for the RAF in the Battle of Britain.
- 27th September: pact signed by Germany, Italy and Japan.
- 7th October: Germany invades Romania.
- 28th October: Italy invades Greece and Albania.
- 20th November: Hungary joins the Axis of Germany, Italy and Japan.
- 23rd November: Romania joins the Axis.
- December: as air raids continue on London, Britain begins the desert offensive against Italy in North Africa.

We hardly knew there was a war on! Newspapers were very thin and only printed edited versions of what was going on. One day in 1940, I was returning home with a friend when we heard an aircraft overhead. We had already volunteered for aircrew and were attending aircraft recognition classes in our enthusiasm. "A short-nosed Blenheim," opined my mate knowledgeably, but the next second we saw the swastika and a stream of bombs descending through the air. Luckily for us, there were very few enemy aircraft over

Harrogate, though the office windows imploded one day a few feet from where I was standing – which was to be one of many narrow escapes for me.

Most of the time, however, the war seemed to be a long way off to us, ex-Londoners. Dunkirk had been evacuated, though I didn't really understand the full significance of this. Churchill became Prime Minister and immediately made Lord Beaverbrook head of the new Ministry of Aircraft Production. Beaverbrook decided that as things were quiet in the capital, he'd bring some sections of The Air Ministry back to London. Just as the exodus from Harrogate began, so did the Blitz, so everyone returned to Harrogate. *As you were!*

Against this to-ing and fro-ing of personnel, I met my future wife. A girl I was dating worked in the Contracts branch of the Air Ministry. One evening I was walking her home through a downpour to Starbeck, an area on the outskirts of Harrogate and she lent me her umbrella for the long wet walk back to my billet. As she was going back to London the next day, she suggested I return the umbrella to a friend of hers who worked in the same department and was due to return to the capital the following week. They'd been at school together and lived in the same area of London. This was how I met Betty. The first girlfriend opted to stay in London with her family, but Betty came back to Harrogate and we started dating. Her digs were also in Starbeck, as bad luck would have it, so I had more long walks at the end of our evenings out. I used to leave the bag with my dance shoes tucked under a hedge in someone's front garden to collect on the way back!

In the winter of 1940 I sustained a football injury which could have jeopardised my future health, but by luck rather than judgment, it didn't. My knee got kicked instead of the ball – and swelled up, well... like a football. There was no A & E in those days, but eventually I saw a doctor who advised me to rest in bed for two weeks. I remember reading *Gone with the Wind* during this enforced rest, and *Tomorrow is another day* etc. Unfortunately, when I got up, I found I couldn't put my foot on the ground. It turned out that the patella had been broken and had set wrongly so I went to hospital where I should have been in the first place. I ended up on crutches, going through a long course of painful manipulation. Cycling helped, too, but the best treatment turned out to be a trip to see Arsenal in the Cup Final, being played at Blackburn Rovers ground! Not the most sensible of decisions, looking back, as I was still on crutches and far from mobile, but my mates promised to help me. Attempting to leave early after the match in order to avoid the crush, we failed, and I got pinioned against a fence in a corner. Almost fainting, I got back to the train station with a lot of help from my friends. What an idiot I'd been, undoing weeks of rehabilitation! The miracle was that when I got up the next morning, I could walk perfectly and something seemed to have righted itself! To this day my dodgy knee has given me no more problems.

I even took up golf as two Scots friends introduced me to the local golf club which offered good rates to the Air Ministry. When one of them was called up, he passed his membership and clubs over to me. Eventually I got my own set of clubs and when I joined the RAF, I left them for safekeeping with my landlady, Hetty. They're probably still in the attic at 46 Franklin Road!

As more and more men were called up, I advanced, career-wise, and was given more responsibility, so I soon became one of the more experienced staff, rather than the junior clerk. The job changed, too, with wartime, and there was a sense of urgency. More initiative – *thinking out of the box,* we'd call it today – was required to get all the supplies we needed from different manufacturers, who were often short of materials, themselves to make their products. Sometimes I travelled to get contracts, and I remember being sent to Coventry (literally) on the day after the heavy bombing, now part of history, which destroyed the cathedral and much else besides. Occasionally I went home to Camberley on leave: arriving in London was a shock and one time reaching Kings Cross Station late at night, I found that no taxis were venturing south of the river in the raids as it was much too dangerous. But the Tube was still running and I got home eventually.

Significant events of WW2
1941

- January: victory in Tobruk in North Africa for Britain and Australia.
- February: under General Rommel the first units of German Afrika Korps arrive in Tripoli.
- March: British forces arrive in Greece.
- April: Germany invades Greece and Yugoslavia and both countries surrender.

- May: the British counter-attack (Operation Brevity) begins in Egypt.
- 24th and 27th May: British ship, *Hood*, sunk by the *Bismarck* and then the *Bismarck* is sunk by the British Navy.
- 8th June: the Allies invade Syria and Lebanon.
- 22nd June: Operation Barbarossa begins with Germany's attack on the Soviet Union.
- 10th July: Germans invade Ukraine. Meanwhile a Mutual Assistance agreement is made between Britain and the Soviets.
- 31st July: instructions go out from Hitler and Goering to prepare the *Final Solution*.
- 20th August: Siege of Leningrad begins.
- 3rd September: first experimental use of gas chambers at Auschwitz.
- 2nd October: Germans advance on Moscow (Operation Typhoon).
- 13th November: British aircraft carrier, *Ark Royal*, is sunk by U-boat off Gibraltar.
- 7th December; Japan attacks Pearl Harbour, American naval base, declaring war on USA and Britain. The next day President Roosevelt declares war on the Axis, then Italy and Germany declare war on the US.
- 25th December: Britain surrenders Hong Kong to the Japanese.

My safe existence lasted until June 1942 when I was called up, and my RAF training began.

I had already volunteered for the RAF and aircrew. It's worth remembering that in those days every member of RAF aircrew was a volunteer. The process had already started and I'd been to RAF Padgate, near Warrington, to take some exam papers and for the required medical, which I passed, in spite of worries about the knee injury.

The days of my misspent youth in Harrogate, trying every exotic drink in Hales bar, were coming to an end. The Air Ministry football and cricket teams were suffering, depleted of men. But if it hadn't been for the war, I'd still have been living at home, commuting into the office. I'd grown up quickly and learnt to stand on my own two feet. I think initially we were less worldly-wise than the very clued-up teenagers of today, but that changed rapidly. A steep learning curve for most of my generation. My younger brother, as I've already said, had already left school and joined the RAF for an apprenticeship as an aero-engineer. He was then to sign on, aged 18, for twelve years, and we were to meet up next in Canada, but that's another story.

At the end of June, 1942, I got my call-up papers.

Why did I volunteer for Aircrew? Well, in my case there were three reasons:

1. Sibling rivalry. My younger brother had stolen a march on me. He was now training to be a pilot after his initial apprenticeship. I didn't want to be left behind.
2. Bed-linen. From working in the equipment branch of the Air Ministry, I knew that aircrew, at the

permanent bases at least, had sheets on their beds. This struck me as a very civilised plus factor.

3. Glamour. Of course. If you were successful at the end of training for aircrew you would get your wings and your *brevet*. You'd at least become a sergeant and you might be commissioned. This all represented a monetary advantage as well.

These were the main motivating factors in my teenage decision to volunteer for aircrew. You didn't think at that stage of where it might lead. Or what might be involved. Or how it would end.

* * *

Believe it or not, the Aircrew Receiving Centre, to which I was told to report, was somewhere already familiar… Lords Cricket Ground! I'd been to county and test matches before the war, but here I was, actually stepping inside the hallowed space of the pavilion. I had my first medical in the Long Room, my first pay parade by the grandstand and my first gas-mask drill down at the Nursery End.

Once the military regime got going, the novelty soon wore off!

Lots of drill. Uniform fitting. Vaccinations and inoculations. After three weeks in elegant billets around St John's Wood and Regent's Park, we were moved on for further training to sleep under canvas on a farm near Ludlow, Shropshire, for Aircrew Camp. There were no facilities and we shaved in a stream at the bottom of a field.

Incredible as it may seem, the recruitment situation then was such that, even though there were huge RAF aircrew losses suffered every day at that stage of the war, there were so many volunteers, almost too many to deal with, that the whole process was being deliberately slowed. All sorts of extras were invented as a kind of toughening-up exercise for the new recruits; for example, at our camp, we were given the task of building a road across the farmer's field, though we weren't sure he really needed one! It was definitely hard work in the heat of the sun, especially if you weren't used to manual labour. There was a *Catch 22* situation regarding a pass-out for the evening: you had to go via the guard room where permission was denied if you had dust on your boots. Well, of course we had dust on our boots... so no one was allowed out! You could call it a boot camp, in both senses of the phrase.

Then I was sent to Scarborough for an initial training course. This was familiar ground: another Yorkshire seaside town where all the hotels were requisitioned for billets. I was in the Prince of Wales Hotel on the sea front. One night, on fire-fighting duty, I found a cache of pre-war chamber pots, all monogrammed with the fleur-de-lys and redolent (sic) of a different era! Of course, we weren't far from Harrogate which suited me down to the ground as I could see Betty and look up any friends who were still there.

The discipline was strict for the three months we spent there, but I can honestly say that when I left I was the fittest I'd ever been. Which certainly helped when running from the cinema to be in by 10pm, the curfew. We did PT on the road, as there wasn't much traffic about, much to the amusement of the holiday-makers who enjoyed the moments when the drill sergeants used choice vocabulary to describe our efforts. We marched everywhere – at speed: 140 paces to the minute, which is almost running. We even marched to and from the education building where we went for all the theory lessons in meteorology, navigation and aircraft recognition.

On one occasion, coming back to the hotel at the usual speed, we found we were expected to go on a cross-country run. A friend and I, being less than keen, decided to skulk in our first-floor room and take an over-long time to change into PT kit, in the hope of avoiding the run. Just as we were congratulating ourselves on this ruse, one of the officers strode in and demanded to know what we were doing, though, of course, he knew perfectly well. "Off you go," he barked, over-riding our pathetic excuses about needing the toilet, "and if you're not in the first twelve at the finish, you're in trouble!"

We could just see the others disappearing over Oliver's Mount; there was no choice but to try and catch them up. We managed personal bests and were placed in the first twelve, to be met by the same supercilious officer, a stereotype beloved in war films. He so enjoyed telling us that we'd qualified for the cross-country team and would have to give up our Saturday afternoon to run in the local championships.

That taught me a lesson! But the three months' training in Scarborough was good and I learnt a lot in spite of, or because of, the tough discipline.

The flying began at last!

I was posted to what was called *grading school*, because this was where you were assessed for pilot or other aircrew training. I was based at Kingston, just outside Carlisle (no.15 E.F.T.S. – Elementary Flight Training School). The accommodation was basic, once again, and by now the winter had set in. I think I was the coldest I've ever been in my life! One Sunday, instead of lying around relaxing on our day of rest, we put all our flying clothes on and got into our beds. And we were still freezing!

We trained on Tiger Moths. I was part of a contingent regularly transported over the border to Scotland to a grass airfield near Gretna Green for 12 hours' flying lessons. You went up in a dual-control plane with an instructor for what was called *circuits and bumps* – says it all really! This consisted of take-offs, landings and short local flights, learning the idiosyncrasies of the Tiger Moth.

One Friday, as I headed for dispersal, the instructor kept me back and said the words, at once exciting and terrifying: "*No, you stay behind – you're going solo.*" Not everyone got this chance during training so I must have shown some aptitude. I took off, flew around for 15 minutes on a designated route, and made a good landing. I was elated. I had solo-ed, in aircraft T6810, as my log-book testifies. And at that stage in my life, I hadn't even driven a motor car…

Unfortunately, I messed up my final training flight and test with the Chief Flying Officer. It was a disaster. When we took off, the plane slewed to starboard and I cottoned on rather late to the fact that the officer was doing this deliberately to test my reactions. Apparently they were too slow. Once up in the air, you had to go into a spin – which Tiger Moths are good at – and then get the plane out of it safely, according to a set procedure. I started to climb, reduced speed, deliberately stalled the engine… so far so good. I used the rudders as I'd been taught, and the plane came out of its spin. But my examiner's damning words were: "Didn't think much of that! The plane got itself out of that spin, not you!"

With this negative verdict ringing in my ears, I went off on Xmas leave, 1942, and afterwards reported to Heaton Park, near Manchester to be told the results of my assessment. I wasn't surprised to learn that I had not been selected to continue as a pilot, but had been chosen to train as a navigator and wireless operator.

Significant events of WW2
1943

- 10th January: Soviets begin an offensive against the Germans at Stalingrad.
- 14th January: President Roosevelt demands unconditional surrender at the Casablanca Conference.
- 2nd February: Germans surrender at Stalingrad, their first major defeat. Soviets recapture Kursk, Rostov and Kharkov.
- 2nd March: Allied victory in North Africa as Germany withdraws from Tunisia. Allies then launch an invasion of Italy.

- July: Allied landings in Sicily (Operation Husky) and bombing offensives on Germany.
- 8th September: Italy surrenders and four days later Mussolini is rescued by the Germans and sets up a Fascist government again.
- 1st October: the Allies enter Naples.
- 13th October: Italy declares war on Germany.
- November: the Allied leaders meet at Teheran and the Soviets recapture Kiev.

I was sent off to do two courses, signals and navigation.

Before these, another interim toughening-up course awaited me in Filey, an RAF regimental base, where I spent my 21st birthday watching demo exercises involving live ammunition and then lying on the ground in deep snow, with my gas mask on, trying to fire at a target. Cold, wet and all too aware that I was dealing with real weaponry, this was definitely not how I'd have chosen to celebrate my coming of age.

From there I went to 1 Radio School, Cranwell, to be taught everything there was to know about radios, the start of my love/hate relationship with them, I might add. You had to learn to operate a Marconi wireless set, and to receive and transmit in Morse code. For days on end we listened to Morse code being sent on a machine for us to decode and had to get up to speed, able to take down 26 words a minute. The concentration needed is so intense that you can only keep this up for a while before you lose it completely. The next stage was learning to send Morse code, at the same speed, with little gaps in transmission so the words made sense and didn't run together. Then there was *fault-finding*, in other words learning everything about the set and all the stuff that could go wrong; not being a natural at electronics, I had to work really hard at this in order to pass. But I did pass out at Cranwell, gaining the little sparks symbol on my sleeve to show I was a wireless-operator.

As for the navigation course, the chances of being sent abroad to take this were high: all the available British airfields were needed for operational purposes by the RAF and the American Air Force. Not to mention the fact that the slower training aircraft would be highly vulnerable to German attack. Usually you went to Canada, Rhodesia or South Africa. It was supposed to be a big secret, not to be imparted to anyone – *careless talk costs lives*, as the slogan went. I was told I was going to Canada and immediately kitted out. As Canada is very cold compared with the other two countries, your destination was pretty obvious to all who saw you in your new togs, i.e. your *Irvine* jacket and twin flying suits: "Oh, I see you're off to Canada!" my landlady announces as soon as I return to my billet.

Canada: August 1943-June 1944

We travelled by train up the west coast to Greenock, in Scotland, where we boarded the pre-war cruise-liner, *Aquitania*, stripped of all its fancy bits, for the week's crossing of the Atlantic. They used large ships like the *Aquitania* and the *Queen Mary* as they were faster and better able to avoid German U-boats. It was a beautiful evening as we sailed down the Clyde looking at the scenery from the deck and mentally saying farewell to the UK, which most of us had never left before. We were not in convoy but for the first two days were shadowed by a Sunderland flying boat, then on our own, then for the last two days we were picked up by an American Air Force Catalina. To our relief, it was an uneventful crossing.

Imagine our surprise when, expecting to make landfall on Canadian shores, we looked out and found we were sailing up the Hudson River by the Statue of Liberty to New York! And what a greeting! Cheering from the dock, people shaking our hands and ladies from all sorts of organisations showering us with cigarettes and chocolates...

Unfortunately there was no time to explore. We took a train up the eastern seaboard to Moncton in New Brunswick. A two-day trip and my first introduction to a sleeper compartment. As we left New York, they were having a blackout practice, but we kept putting the blinds up because we wanted to see the sights.

We eventually arrived in Moncton, a transit base, via the Maritime States. Before you were posted to navigation school, you were kept busy and I did a stint in the admin office, which proved rather useful as I managed to track down my brother. Communication wasn't easy in wartime when you were constantly on the move, but I knew he'd done pilot-training in Detroit, then Pensacola in Florida, before the Americans came into the war. I guessed he must be coming up to the final part of his training but hadn't a clue where he was doing it. Through a bit of research in

Hill.

AIR NAVIGATION SCHOOL.

No. 33 A.N.S, R.A.F., MOUNT HOPE, Hamilton, Ontario.
From.... 20/9/43........ To.... 25/2/44...............

SUBJECT	MARKS Poss.	Obtd.	FLYING TIME ON COURSE. Type of a/c.	Day	Night
AIR NAV ELEM.	200	175	ANSON.	89.15	50.15
AIR NAV THEORY	100	86			
AIR NAV EXERCISES	200	166			
METEOROLOGY	100	69			
SIGNALS (THEORY)	100.	57			
SIGNALS (MORSE)	100.	63			
A/C REC.	50.	48			
RECCO GROUND	50.	41			
PHOTO GROUND	50.	43			
ARMAMENTS.	50	37			
AIR NAV (DAY).	250.	194			
AIR NAV (NIGHT).	150.	119			
LOG KEEPING.	150.	124			
RECCO AIR	100.	85			
PHOTO AIR	100.	93			
SIG. AIR OPERATING	200.	162			
MET. OBS.	50.	45			
TOTAL	2,000.	1607	TOTAL	89.15	50.15
% Obtained		80.3			

REMARKS   PASSED

.... *Aldenett* s/ldr.

for CHIEF INSTRUCTOR.

the office, I found to my delight that he had passed, got his wings, and was doing a reconnaissance course just across the way on Prince Edward Island. I applied for special leave to see Peter and was given three days to go and visit.

I should say at this point, because it's relevant to my financial state, that one of the joys of Moncton was that you could send food parcels home to the UK with all its shortages. So I spent quite a lot of money sending food across the Atlantic to my parents, and to Betty's. I just about had enough cash left to get the ferry across to Prince Edward Island. Peter and a mate met me in Charlottetown. His first words were, "I don't know where you're going to stay tonight because we're stony-broke!"

"Nice to see you again, too, bro!"

I'd been hoping that my brother, being a qualified Sergeant Pilot, would be able to subsidise me. Obviously not.

What followed was a bit like a Whitehall farce, changing clothes in cupboards, not to mention identities. Peter and his mate decided I would wear one of their uniforms and stay on the station with them. I was given a tunic and taken into the mess. Very anxious lest I be discovered – I was just a Leading Aircraftsman at the time – I was introduced all round as the new pilot.

* * *

Looking back I probably didn't stand out at all as it wasn't a permanent base and there were new people going through all the time on short courses. My brother and his mates were thoroughly enjoying the subterfuge, but I wasn't. I didn't find it as funny as they did. What was going to happen on Monday morning when I put my uniform back on – with its white flash showing I was only an aircrew cadet?

I was mightily relieved when the weekend's high jinks came to an end and I managed to get out of the station undetected. On the ferry back I wondered if impersonating another rank was a court-martial offence. It could have been the end of my career!

The post script came a few days later when I was lazing outside my billet on a nice summer's evening. A Sergeant Pilot came up to me and asked if I was Pete Hill's brother. "Good show!" he says. "We wondered if you'd like to come over for dinner in the mess this evening?"

I politely declined the invitation.

* * *

I found I was going to be posted to No. 33 Air Navigation School at Mount Hope, near Hamilton, Ontario.

A lot of the Canadian RAF training bases were in the Prairies, out in the mid- or far-west, i.e. the back-of-beyond, but Hamilton was the fifth largest base in the country, so I was very pleased. The locals call it *The Mount*. It's a steep plateau, yes, but not a mountain by any stretch of the imagination.

I started navigation training with classroom courses in chart-plotting, meteorology, armaments, signalling and aircraft recognition. More practical bits included learning to strip a Browning 303 gun. Then there were the usual sessions of Drill and PT, of course. Winter set in and you knew it'd come to stay. PT became a choice between skating on the outside rink or badminton in one of the hangers. I opted for the latter and became quite good at it, getting to the final of a tournament. Of course, there was also the tough assault-course stuff, crawling through mud, swinging on and off ropes and so on. We even had to give a demo to the locals.

Then there was flying and navigation practice. You learnt a point of navigation then you went up in Ansons to try it out. These slow, stable pre-war planes were ideal to practise on because they took a crew of five or six. You had a staff pilot – the only experienced crew- member – and the rest of us took it in turns as First or Second Navigator, sitting beside him, or Wireless Operator. The Second Navigator's role included map-reading, taking drift readings, recording the weather, wind direction, the amount of cloud and so on. Then there were other essential dogsbody jobs, too, like winding up the undercarriage on some of the very old planes which didn't have automatic retractable ones.

On one flight, I encountered a problem which had nothing to do with navigation and everything to do with the comfort of my own undercarriage. I was getting desperate for a pee! So I left my seat to go in search of the *facilities* which usually consisted of a plastic funnel mid-starboard which went into the fuselage. To my horror I found that this plane had *no* plastic funnel at all! I couldn't last out for another two hours, that much was certain. I went back and bumped into one of my co-trainees having trouble with a TR1184/85 transmitter/receiver wireless, a Heath

Robinson affair, into which you had to insert two coils to get a frequency. Every hour you had to change frequency and call base to get a weather report as snow storms in that part of the world could come out of the blue – literally. This chap was the class idiot who usually managed to get into a fix more times than anyone else. One of the coils had stuck and he was trying unsuccessfully to hack it out with an axe, kept on board in case the plane crashed and you needed to make a swift exit! Not surprisingly, he was far from sympathetic to my predicament.

"Pee on the floor, then!" was his tersely muttered suggestion.

I decided this was not an option, but I think it might have been safer than the one I chose: to urinate out of the starboard door.

I asked the pilot to fly steady and what followed was one of the scariest moments of my whole RAF career. Every time I tried to open the door, it slammed shut in the slipstream from the starboard engine. I soon discovered that I didn't have enough hands. I had to hold the door open, cling to the aircraft for dear life a*nd undo layers of clothing from parachute harness through complete battledress to my inner one-piece flying suit!* If we'd hit an air pocket the door would have been sucked open and I'd have gone out with it. Luckily we didn't.

The relief was amazing.

Of course I got a lot of ribbing later from my friends. One of my best mates, Yorkshireman Charlie Harte, composed an imaginary headline for the local paper. *Biggest icicle in living memory drops from the sky over Ontario!*

The crunch came, of course, when we got into night flying. Much more difficult.

As was our final exercise, which involved multi-tasking, being navigator and wireless operator, the dual role essential for smaller aircraft like Mosquitoes which only held two men, the pilot *and* the navigator/ wireless operator. Having said that, it was relatively straightforward, compared to what we were going to face later when it came to ops over Holland and Germany.

Navigation in that part of Canada should have been easy: as you took off you saw the lights of Hamilton and, over to the east, the lights of Toronto. On a clear night you might even see Detroit lit up on the USA border. So basically you couldn't get lost. But you did! And they were on to you. At the end of each exercise you had a debriefing, and it was soon clear, from your calculations and the chart you'd kept, whether you'd gone where you were supposed to go. You were marked on the accuracy of your flight plan.

For a bit of respite, we found our way to the YMCA on the station, where there was a complete novelty for us – a juke box. One likely lad decided to up the ante when he discovered that you could compress one of the metal buttons on your trousers to just the right size for the slot on the jukebox. When the chap came to empty the juke box, that was the end of the scam, of course. Just as well – we had very few buttons left on our trousers.

On our first 48-hour leave, Charlie and I made for Detroit to explore the city. In the evening, we found another novelty – an all-night cinema. What a brilliant idea to watch movies all night and avoid paying for a hotel! They started with a highly emotional Tallulah Bankhead film which soon became inaudible as loud snores filled the picture-house. We quickly realised that lots of people had just come in to get out of the cold, including large numbers of homeless African Americans who were treating the place as a doss-house. At one point we were politely asked to move seats so that the usherettes could clean the cinema. On leaving at 6am the outside temperature was sub-zero. We decided it had not been such a great idea.

On another 48-hour leave, I travelled to Michigan again, to a lovely place, called Ann Arbor, to meet up with my brother's girlfriend, from when he'd been stationed in Detroit. She agreed to sign a paper and stand surety for me on trips to the States, a bit of red tape required because a few members of ground crew had gone on leave to the USA and never come back! So an eighteen-year-old student at the University of Michigan provided my visa – daft really!

At the YMCA in Ann Arbour, I signed my name, and, without thinking, scribbled *Camberley, London*, underneath. This led to all sorts of questions about how the Brits had coped with the Blitz. Of course, I hadn't experienced any of it so explained how I'd been evacuated to Yorkshire. Then, seeing the white flash in my cap, they asked me all about the combat missions I'd been on. Well, no, I told them, I hadn't actually been on any. Yet. "You damn limeys are so modest!" someone drawled. I realised I could have invented any war experiences I liked, they were so eager for news!

The week before the final exams, I felt that what we didn't know, we never would know, so I suggested to my mate Charlie that we had a weekend in Toronto. I'd met a girl I was seeing there, so that probably had something to do with it. Charlie initially thought we should revise for our exams but changed his mind when I said that my girlfriend had a very attractive sister. We could afford a hotel for the weekend but Charlie, a typical Yorkshireman, suggested we save the money and apply for a billet which would be free. We were allocated a room in someone's home on the edge of town and made very welcome when we went to drop off our bags.

What a memorable weekend! First we went to an ice hockey match at Mapleleaf Gardens, then to one of Isobel's famous parties, Isobel being an émigré Scot who used to host parties for the RAF. Result Charlie got completely blotto and there was no way we'd ever get him back to our billet. "You phone up and apologise," I muttered. "It was your idea to stay out of town!" Fortunately the husband answered the phone and very little explanation was required. He cottoned on immediately and generously asked us to dinner the next day when we went to collect our stuff. The Canadians we met were all so friendly, the hospitality incredible.

Eventually we graduated – or most of us did. Preceding me on the same course was the famous entertainer and comedian, Jimmy Edwards, who, in spite of his M.A. Cantab, failed his navigation, but later went on to become a pilot. In all modesty I have to say that I passed out as the top cadet! I never saw the Honours board with my name at the top, but I felt very proud to march up first, in order of merit, at the Passing Out parade, to collect my brevet from the CO in front of the whole station.

I was also selected for an immediate commission. Which meant I could go to one of the tailors in Hamilton to be measured for my new uniform, and then to Eton's, the main shop there, for shirts, tie, shoes, *not* boots, and a suitcase, not a kit bag. The only downside was that my uniform wasn't ready for immediate leave, so I sewed sergeant stripes and wings onto my usual uniform so at least I could go as an aircrew member.

* * *

If you're detecting a pattern to our brief spells of leave, you'll guess that alcohol, fun and some degree of misadventure were all to play their part in this one, too. Then there was the lure of America. We were all fans of the many glamorous films coming out of Hollywood at the time and, not surprisingly, for graduation leave, we decided to head for New York, which we'd only briefly experienced when we disembarked from the *Aquitania*.

The trip started inauspiciously: we boarded the train for New York, via Niagara and Buffalo, only to be made to get off at the border! This was because Charlie, in his wisdom, had decided that our US 'visas', those fictitious undertakings, were a waste of time and had chucked them away. To quote Oliver Hardy, "This is another fine mess you've gotten me into!"

No. 33 Air Navigation School,
Royal Air Force,
M.P.O. 211,
HAMILTON,
Ontario.

Date _25 Feb. 1944._

NOTIFICATION OF SECTION FOR
APPOINTMENT TO COMMISSIONED RANK.

No _15209/S_ Rank _AC_ Name _HILL. J. H. C._

Notification has been received at this School, Chief
of the Air Staff advice _P.5.186_ dated _24 Feb. 19.44_,
that the marginally noted airman, a graduate of Course No _85B_ _____

No. 33 A.N.S., M.P.O. 211, HAMILTON, Ontario, has been selected for
appointment to commissioned rank, effective _25 Feb_ 19.44.
_____

Signed _R. V. Bakey_ F/O
for Officer Commanding,
No. 33 Air Navigation School,
M.P.O. 211, HAMILTON, Ontario.

We set off through the snow to talk to border control where we got lucky: the Immigration Officer invited us in to get warm and, over hot drinks, offered to fix us a lift into Buffalo in the first car that had space in it.

We finally made it to New York the next day and had a great time. We saw the sights, including *Jack Dempsey's Bar* on Broadway, where we got talking to a couple of Americans with their two daughters, later joining up with a British naval party from a ship in dry dock in Brooklyn. It seemed that everyone was on the town enjoying themselves. Of course, Charlie had too much to drink… again. I should say that he was normally the most friendly, debonair, warm-hearted guy you could imagine, but he was the type who could turn a bit aggressive when drunk. When he asked the band to play *Stardust*, that was always the signal to get him out… fast. The waiters – ex-thugs to be precise – spotted this immediately and gave him an interesting option: leave the club immediately or go downstairs for *treatment*. He chose the latter, undeterred by the prospect and probably too drunk to care. He disappeared for an hour, returning completely sober and looking fresh as a daisy. I wish I knew what they did to him. He didn't remember, of course.

When the money ran out, we spent the rest of our leave with friends of Charlie's parents, who'd emigrated to Stanford, Connecticut. We hadn't actually been to war, but we might as well have been. We were treated royally, entertained, even interviewed by the local paper. Through Charlie's friends, we met an American family, the Smiths; I still write to their daughter, then eight years old, who came downstairs in her pyjamas to play the accordion for us.

When I got back to Mount Hope I collected my new uniform. Not only that, but I was now in the Officers' Mess, not the Airmen's, which took a bit of getting used to to start with.

Where next? The course director had the decision of where to send us all. Some of the married men were repatriated immediately for the next stage of their training, some went on a general reconnaissance course to Prince Edward Island, and the top cadets were to go to an Operational Training Unit in Greenwood, Nova Scotia, to commence training on Mosquito planes. I was thrilled to bits to be selected as aircrew for these already legendary planes which, I knew, were very fast and much easier to manoeuvre in the skies. Many pilots and navigators were keen to join the Mossie squadrons. In 1942 Bomber Command had realised that their results

Mosquito Mk IV with camouflage colours

were not encouraging, and that new aircraft with more precise instruments were needed to replace the pre-1939 designs. The Mosquito was one of the hugely successful, new planes and it was to have a meteoric career in WW2.

The journey to O.T.U. Greenwood took two or three days, via St John to take a ferry across the Bay of Fundy, up to Nova Scotia and finally on to Greenwood.

Shock! Horror! It was completely in the wilds, in the middle nowhere! It turned out that Greenwood had one street, one shop and the railway running through, which went from one end of the state to the other. There was absolutely nowhere to go in the evening, the nearest small town being 11 miles away.

The majority of the planes were, of course, Mosquitoes, though there were a few others, used for non-OTU purposes. For example, while I was waiting to start my course, I did two local flights in a Bolingbroke (a variation of a Blenheim) and two more in an Oxford. The Mosquitoes, themselves, were Canadian-built, under licence from De Havilland. They had American Packard engines, instead of the British Merlin, and a Bendix radio – another set for me to get to grips with.

The Mosquito was a fast plane, which could do up to, and sometimes over, 388mph, faster than the Spitfire. It was streamlined, compact, and beautifully designed. Sometimes called the plane that saved Britain, it was dual-purpose, used for reconnaissance missions as well as combat. The basic shape changed little, through the various models produced, and only had slight variations according to different additions and installations. The protruding guns

No. 36 O.T.U?

S I G N A L S

Equipment used in the air :- T1154/R1155
TA-12c/RA-1QDB, VHF R/T, SCR522A/TR1133c

Air Exercises :-

H/F Homings ....
M/F Bearings ....
Loop Bearings ....
Assessments :-
Practical Ground ..... 75% ....
" " Air ..... 80 ....
Morse Speed .... 20 .... wpm
Visual (Aldis) Speed .... 8 .... wpm

General assessment as W/OPr. :-
...... *Above Average* ....

Remarks ....

....

....

...... *Bell* .... P/o
f .... Station Signals Officer

Date	Hour	Aircraft Type and No.	Pilot	Duty
Summary for		Lee "Louise"	1944	1. Total Lee 10:05 ✓
Unit		Anson John. 15 O.T.U.	Aircraft	2. Total M.R. 10:25 ✓
Date		3rd August, 1944	Types Anson	3.
Signature		Lee.		4. Grand Total 20:30 ✓

D.S. Fuller.

F/L. O/c Anson John.

Lee

W/Cdr. C.I. B.O.T.U.

THESE PHOTOGRAPHS, IN CIVILIAN CLOTHES, WERE TAKEN
FOR USE IN IDENTIFICATION PAPERS IN THE EVENT OF
BEING SHOT DOWN OVER ENEMY TERRITORY AND,
HOPEFULLY, ESCAPING BEING A P.O.W AND BEING
ASSISTED BY THE RESISTANCE ORGANISATION.

Photos for use in ID papers in the event of being shot down over enemy territory and trying to evade capture on some models were the only things which marred the perfectly neat, rounded lines of the plane, and took away from the simple *toy* plane appearance. Initially painted yellow, then black, they were, of course, made of wood, but because they were so tough and sturdy, you forget all about this fact. They had a personality all their own, and the two-man crews of pilot and navigator came to appreciate their strength and reliability.

The system was that you were expected to crew up at the beginning of the course in order to start flying. If you've read about the random, sort-yourself-out method of crewing up for RAF fighter planes in WW2, it wasn't a fiction. During the evenings in the Mess at Greenwood, the new intake of pilots would size up the new intake of navigators and get together over a pint to select their flying partner. A bit like waiting to be picked for a team at school. In the larger planes you would need a *team*, but, of course, the Mozzie cockpit only held two men. Thus the dice of fate were rolled. I'm the son of Irish parents and I definitely got lucky, though it didn't seem so at the time. I went down with a bad case of tonsillitis and I was confined to the sick bay, for the first crewing up. So I had to wait till the next intake of pilots to come along.

One evening, in the Mess, a Canadian Flight Lieutenant, an experienced pilot, came over and asked if I was Johnny Hill and politely invited me to be his navigator. That was my first introduction to Courtney (Court) Shippey Spurr Gilliatt, with whom I was to fly until the end of the war. We became firm friends, but that simple phrase understates the incredible relationship of trust and interdependence which built up between many a pilot and navigator, flying wartime missions. Because there were only two of you in the Mosquito cockpit, going through the gamut of experiences and emotions together, the close relationship which developed over time was a unique one, different again from those amongst larger crews in other combat aircraft.

We were immediately started on night flights. There were few lights to help and you could get atrocious weather conditions, too. An incident with another crew acted as a lesson to be extra careful – always. Their plane had overshot the base and was heading straight out into the Atlantic, very low on fuel by then: the navigator panicked, especially when he radioed base for the homing signal, but couldn't hear them. They could hear him, but they had to send up another Mossie so as to relay messages and get the plane and its crew home.

On one night flight over New Brunswick, Court and I went into a rainstorm and very heavy cloud cover. As a navigator, I could pinpoint our route but charting it with maximum precision wouldn't help in these conditions; I still had to make extra sure that, when we eventually came out of the cloud, we were not over high ground and imminently in danger of crashing. I decided to use my initiative and my radio skills to make certain we were OK. We had a new type of radio set, an American V/Bendix, on board so I'd had to learn a new system. As I'd lost the signal from base, I decided to change frequency. In my billet, I'd got interested in following ice hockey matches on Radio Moncton and I knew that, when there was a break for adverts, they sent out a call sign. If I could pick up their signal, I could home in on it. The little screen on my set had two arrows on it and when they met I knew I was over the station, over Moncton. The relief was huge: this wasn't in the training manual, but thinking out of the box had worked.

Back at base we had to make our own entertainment. Soon after arriving in Canada, I had become aware that the laws regarding the purchase and consumption of alcohol were different from those in Britain, and were further complicated by not being the same everywhere in the country, each province having its own regulations. In Ontario, for example, there had been a registration system, which we could join as operational trainees, whereby you had to apply at your local liquor store for a permit, costing a dollar, which entitled you to buy your prescribed ration once a month. When our graduation dinner in Hamilton drew near, we'd had to deposit our allowances at the Royal Connaught Hotel to be held there so as to ensure that we had enough alcohol for the occasion!

In Quebec, in French Canada, you could get liquor anywhere, but Nova Scotia was a dry state and alcohol was only available on a doctor's prescription. There were no pubs! Fortunately, Greenwood was an RAF station so the liquor flowed.

One weekend the stations across the whole country were open to the public, holding various functions to raise money to build more Mosquitoes and Spitfires. As we were out in the middle of nowhere, I was of the opinion that no one would bother to come and visit us, but I'd reckoned without the licensing laws. Everyone in the state knew we were a source of alcohol, so the world came to Greenwood, travelling in anything from horse-drawn farm carts to cars and trucks. Whole families stayed on into the evening, when we'd organised a dance. What with the profit on drinks and the charge of 25 cents a go on the dance floor, we ended up as the highest revenue raiser in the country!

There was also sport, of course. I remember playing in some inter-station football match and shoulder-charging one of the opposite team. One of their supporters protested loudly against my tactics: "You dirty bastard!" he called out loudly, adding, "Sir!" a few seconds later.

The afterthought caused much laughter from the immediate spectators.

* * *

Eventually the training course ended and I passed out as the top navigator again!

We were going to be repatriated, sailing from Halifax, NS, on board the *New Amsterdam*, a huge Dutch liner, carrying army as well as RAF forces. It took three days to get everyone, plus kit and stores, on board. We were all sleeping in hammocks and one Canadian *penguin*, a non-flying officer, was terribly seasick immediately. On the third day of boarding, he estimated that we were halfway across the Atlantic, a thought which gave him some small amount of comfort. We hadn't the heart to tell him we were still in port, though he found out soon enough. When we were eventually approaching the coast of Scotland, I told various friends I'd made on board, that the scenery sailing up the Clyde was the best ever. We arrived in fog and couldn't see a thing.

The New Amsterdam

NO. 16. MOSQUITO COURSE. A.SQUAD.
P/o Bulmer.   P/o.Mallet.
    Sgt Parfitt. Sgt. Lunn. P/o Young. P/o.Miller P/o.Campbell. Sgt.Gubbins. Sgt. Whately.
                                                                        Knight.
    P/o Binion F/o. Nairn. F/o.Pearce. F/L Webb F/o Carvosso. P/o Voss   F/Sgt. Baird.
                                                                EXTREME RIGHT.
                                                                        P/o Hill.

Back in Blighty: June 1944

Once ashore, things moved fast. The navigators were sent to – guess where – Harrogate, while the Canadian pilots went to Bournemouth on embarkation leave, so Court and I were split. Ours not to reason why. As you might imagine, I was happy to have some leave in Harrogate, knowing the town, as I did, but my social life was soon to be cut short. In early July 1944, a dramatic knock on the door and a policeman handing me a telegram, recalled me to duties at 13 O.T.U. Bicester. There, incidentally, I was given my own batman to make my bed and polish my shoes. Court soon arrived and we started night flying our favourite plane for the first time in England. On the downside, we were flying in blackout conditions with no lights to pinpoint our route. On the plus side was the fact that the new model of Mosquito at this base had radar installed! There was no radio! After all the tussles I'd had with different radio sets, getting to know their idiosyncrasies, I found the radar set built in at the back of the armour-plating behind Court's seat. There was no way you could get to it to do any maintenance: if it packed up, it packed up! But it was to make a huge difference.

We flew various routes over the UK, using radar as the main navigation aid. Preparing to land at Bicester we always looked for a red signal light on top of a nearby church spire, but one night Court was worried when I told him we were over the airfield because he couldn't see the light. Nor could I. So we flew around again while I rechecked. After three more circuits, I was absolutely sure I was correct and we went in to land – safely – on the airfield. It turned out that the red light had been switched off because there was a German night fighter in the area. I was less anxious about the enemy plane and more concerned about the accuracy of my navigation.

FESTIVE FLASHBACK

It's November 1941. The festive season is ushered in early for men in training at No. 33 air navigation school, R.A.F. Mount Hope. They are entertained at a Christmas dinner in St. Stephen's parish hall. Tables are laden with good things and the menu includes turkey, plum pudding and all the trimmings. Rev. Canon John Samuel and Mrs. Samuel preside. The guests, all from overseas, thoroughly enjoy the repast and the entertainment that follows.

FORM 1767

ROYAL AIR FORCE

NAVIGATOR'S, AIR BOMBER'S AND
AIR GUNNER'S FLYING LOG BOOK

164043

915 Hill

Name

The following pages from my logbook show my wartime 'ops' clearly numbered and underlined in red.

167 SQUADRON, LASHAM

Date	Hour	Aircraft Type and No.	Pilot	Duty	Remarks (including results of bombing, gunnery, exercises, etc.)	Time carried forward	Flying Times Day	Night
		Mosquito				201.50		73.55
SEPTEMBER 1944								
17.44	17.30	C	F/Lt GILLIATT	NAVIGATOR	LOCAL FLYING FAMILIARISATION		.15	
18.44	14.00	HR 195	F/Lt GILLIATT	NAVIGATOR	N.F.T.		.30	
19.44	14.?	NS 934	F/Lt GILLIATT	NAVIGATOR	N.F.T.		.20	
20.44	15.30	HR 239	F/Lt GILLIATT	NAVIGATOR	N.F.T. PRACTICE BOMBING		.40	
21.44	15.30	NT 226	F/Lt GILLIATT	NAVIGATOR	N.F.T		.10	
22.44	16.10	HR 254	F/Lt GILLIATT	NAVIGATOR	N.F.T PRACTICE BOMBING		.55	
23.44	20.10	"	F/Lt GILLIATT	NAVIGATOR ①	OP.. PATROL of VENLO REFORMED COLOGNE DÜSSELDORF AREA Dun. to la JONCTAS			3.40
24.44	11.50	"	F/Lt GILLIATT	NAVIGATOR	BONIFACE - BASE (Undercarriage collapsed on landing)		.10	
25.44	14.50	PZ 336	F/Lt GILLIATT	NAVIGATOR	N.F.T		.20	
26.44	16.15	NS 934	F/Lt GILLIATT	NAVIGATOR	N.F.T PRACTICE BOMBING		.45	
					TOTAL TIME ...205.55			77.35

Time carried forward :— 2 rods ... 71.35

Flying Times	
Day	Night

Date	Hour	Aircraft Type and No.	Pilot	Duty	Remarks (including results of bombing, gunnery, exercises, etc.)	Day	Night

SUMMARY FOR SEPT 1944 (107 Sqn.)

	Day	Night
H/C MOSQUITO	4 05	3 40

UNIT - 107 SQDN.
DATE - 2nd Oct 1944
SIGNATURE: [illegible]

Oct 1944		MOSQUITO					
3rd	14.30	HR 247	F/Lt ELLIOTT	NAVIGATOR	N.F.T.	.20	
5th	21.30	HR 247	F/Lt ELLIOTT	NAVIGATOR ②	OP'S - PATROL of AMECK ICE FELT MEERSEN		3.55
					WESEL- EMLMEN - STADT STERMEN		
13th	04.15	6 (Pz 225)	F/Lt ELLIOTT	NAVIGATOR ③	OP'S - PATROL of BREMEN. FLUSHING fongs		2.30
					Also from KNOCKE along some line to FLUSHINE to		
14th	17.00	Pz 225	F/Lt ELLIOTT	NAVIGATOR ④	N.F.T.	.40	
16th	20.30	Pz 225	F/Lt ELLIOTT	NAVIGATOR	OP'S - PATROL of ALKMAAR - HAGUE - INTERCEPTION - SCHIPHOL - LEEUWARDEN		3.20
					LEEUWARDEN- LEEUWARDEN- STAVEREN- ENKHUIZEN- HAGUE- AMSTERDAM		
					HAARLEM - ALKMAAR		
19th	15.30	HX 465	F/Lt ELLIOTT	NAVIGATOR	N.F.T.	.20	

Total Time ... Dot . 15. 81. 20

HARTFORD BRIDGE

257

Time carried forward:- 210.20 / 87.20

Date	Hour	Aircraft Type and No.	Pilot	Duty	Remarks (including results of bombing, gunnery, exercises, etc.)	Day	Night
Nov 1944							
1st	15.30	HR 360	F/Lt Gilliatt	Navigator	N.F.T.	.35	
2nd	12.40	HR 350	F/Lt Gilliatt	Navigator	N.F.T.	.40	
2nd	20.10	HR 350	F/Lt Gilliatt	Navigator ⑤	(P) Patrol of Willemstad, Rotterdam, Haverlem, Amersfoort, Veenendaal, Zutphen, Wilhelmstad)		3.00
4/5	22.45	HR 350	F/Lt Gilliatt	Navigator ⑥	(P) Patrol of Emmerich, Weel, Munster. ONABRUCK		3.50
6th	16.30	HR 350	F/Lt Gilliatt	Navigator	N.F.T.	.40	
8/9	23.00	HR 350	F/Lt Gilliatt	Navigator ⑦	(P) Patrol of Harderwirk, Amersfoort, Devenver, Zutphen, Arnheim, Zaltbommel, Jutterson, Utrecht		3.30
9th	15.15	HR 350	F/Lt Gilliatt	Navigator	N.F.T.	.45	
10th	16.30	Hx 965	F/Lt Gilliatt	Navigator	N.F.T.	.10	
1st	16.40	HR 350	F/Lt Gilliatt	Navigator	N.F.T	.15	
30th	11.05 / 12.10	OXFORD 3600	F/Lt Potter, W/Cdr Satt	Passenger	Hartford Bridge Latham, Latham Edinoy	.10 / 1.25	

Total Time ...295.00 / 91.40

CAMBRAI / EPINOY FRANCE

Date	Hour	Aircraft Type and No.	Pilot	Duty		Remarks (including results of bombing, gunnery, exercises, etc)	Time carried forward — 915.00 97.10	
				Day	Night		Flying Times	
							Day	Night
			(107 Sqdn)					
			SUMMARY FOR NOV. 1944	Day	Night			
		A/C:- MOSQUITO	2.05	10.20				
		OXFORD	1.35					
		UNIT:- 107 Sqdn.						
		DATE:- 2nd Dec 1944						
		SIGNATURE:- _illegible_			Mallam F/L. o/c A Flight		
						signature F/Lt W/Cdr o/c 107 Sqdn.		
1st DEC. 1944		H.R.350 MOSQUITO	F/Lt GILLIATT	NAVIGATOR		N.F.T.	.45	
3rd		H.R.350	F/Lt GILLIATT	NAVIGATOR. ⑧		OPs. Patrol of railway from HARPS HERFORD. Returned ... from patrol area ...		2.30
4th		H.R.350	F/Lt GILLIATT	NAVIGATOR		N.F.T.	.30	
5th		H.R.350	F/Lt GILLIATT	NAVIGATOR		N.F.T.	.10	
6th		H.R.350	F/Lt GILLIATT	NAVIGATOR ⑨		OPs. Patrol of HEINSBERG, BARDIKS, NUSSBAUM. On WESEL to ... KEVELAER to.		2.00
7th		H.R.350	F/Lt GILLIATT	NAVIGATOR		N.F.T.	.15	
7th		H.R.350	F/Lt GILLIATT	NAVIGATOR ⑩		OPs. Stocks in barracks and buildings in GAIKRATH ...		1.50
						TOTAL TIME 916.30 104.00		

Time carried forward :— 216.20 | 104.00

DETACHMENT (cont.) MOSQUITO

Date	Hour	Aircraft Type and No.	Pilot	Duty	Remarks (including results of bombing, gunnery, exercises, etc.)	Flying Times Day	Night
9th.		H.R. 350	F/O GILLIATT	NAVIGATOR	N.F.T.	.10	
11th.		H.R. 350	F/O GILLIATT	NAVIGATOR	N.F.T. Low level formation Cross Country	1.00	
11th.		H.R. 350	F/O GILLIATT	NAVIGATOR ⑪	OPS. Strike on WAGENRIEGE. Fires left burning in target area		1.55
12th.		H.R. 350	F/O GILLIATT	NAVIGATOR	N.F.T.	.20	
17th.		H.R. 350	F/O GILLIATT	NAVIGATOR ⑫	OPS. Patrol of railway between LEER MEPPEN LINGEN. RHEINE. MUNSTER		3.15
18th.		H.R. 350	F/O GILLIATT	NAVIGATOR ⑬	N.F.T.	.40	
23rd.	02.15	H.R. 350	F/O GILLIATT	NAVIGATOR ⑬	OPS. Patrol of NUNKWEILER - MÜHLENBACH ULMEN area. Diverted to VITRY		1.45
23/24th	01.40	H.R. 350	F/O GILLIATT	NAVIGATOR ⑭	OPS. Patrol of STADTKYLL - BONN - MAYEN area		2.05
24th.	17.55	H.R. 350	F/O GILLIATT	NAVIGATOR ⑮	OPS. Patrol of NEUERBACH FISCO AMMENBACH ADENAU MAYEN WITTLICH VIRARSEN area		1.45
24.25 th	23.20	H.R. 350	F/O GILLIATT	NAVIGATOR ⑯	OPS. (Turn.bout) Patrol of NEUERBACH FISCO BUSENBACH ARENKWEILER MAYEN WITTLICH VIRARSEN area		1.40

Total Time ...... 218.40 | 116.25

Time carried forward :— ...218 Hrs 116:35

Date	Hour	Aircraft Type and No.	Pilot	Duty	Remarks (Including results of bombing, gunnery, exercises, etc.)	Flying Times Day	Night
Dec 1944 (cont.)		MOSQUITO					
29.12	15.10	HR 356	F/Lt ELLIATT	NAVIGATOR	N.F.T.	.15	
30.12	20.30	HR 356	F/Lt EWIATT	NAVIGATOR (17)	OPS - Patrol of GEREUX - BULLINGEN - PRUM - HOUFFALIZE area		1.50
31.12	15.10	HR 356	F/Lt ELLIATT	NAVIGATOR	N.F.T.	.30	
31.12	22.10	HR 356	F/Lt ELLIATT	NAVIGATOR (18)	Ops - Patrol of DINAN - MAYEN - EUSKIRCHEN ZULPICH, GERMUND - BRUN		1.55

Summary for Dec 1944   (107 Sqdn)

	Day	Night
	4.25	22.30

A/C MOSQUITO
UNIT 107 SQDN
DATE 1st Jan 1945
Signature...

M.Allard S/Ldr of. A Flight

NLCMR of 107 SQDN

Total Time ...219.25 126.10

Date	Hour	Aircraft Type and No.	Pilot	Duty	Remarks (including results of bombing, gunnery, exercises, etc.)	Day	Night
					Time carried forward :- 27.9.25		120.40
Jan 1945		MOSQUITO					
1st	21.00	HR 350	F/Lt Gilliatt	Navigator ⑲	Ops:- Patrol of enemy positions in front. Trouble in vicinity of ST VITH HOUFFALIZE		2.30
6th	05.25	HR 350	F/Lt Gilliatt	Navigator ⑳	Ops:- Strike on railway targets north of rft by fog at BORINCHEM. Midlands covered. Left flat encumbered		1.45
7th	15.16	HR 350	F/Lt Gilliatt	Navigator ㉑	N.F.T.	30	
9th	14.40	HR 350	F/Lt Gilliatt	Navigator ㉒	N.F.T.	.15	.15
16th	19.00	HR 350	F/Lt Gilliatt	Navigator ㉓	Ops:- Weather. Returned to Base due to instrument failure.		
17th	15.00	HR 350	F/Lt Gilliatt	Navigator ㉔	N.F.T.	.20	
17th	18.35	HR 350	F/Lt Gilliatt	Navigator ㉕	Ops:- Strike on NEBBRE. to ind Sr over target to bombed on instruments		1.50
19th	14.30	HR 350	F/Lt Gilliatt	Navigator ㉖	N.F.T.	1.00	
19th	17.30	HR 350	F/Lt Gilliatt	Navigator ㉗	Ops:- Strike on ERKELENZ. Dio long fin burning when target left		2.10
20th	03.45	HR 350	F/Lt Gilliatt	Navigator ㉘	Ops:- Strike on ERKELENZ		1.50
					Total Time	121.30	130.30

Time carried forward— 223.45 | 130.40

Date	Hour	Aircraft Type and No.	Pilot	Duty	Remarks (including results of bombing, gunnery, exercises, etc.)	Day	Night
FEB 1945							
6th	12.00	DAKOTA		PASSENGER	NORTHOLT- BRUSSELS- VITRY	2.30	
7th	15.40	MOSQUITO HR 730	F/Lt GILLIATT	NAVIGATOR	N.F.T.	.25	
8th	00.20	HR 350	F/Lt GILLIATT	NAVIGATOR (24)	OPS Patrol of rail and road movement in area ROERMOND- VENLO- AFFEREN- MILLINGEN- REES- RHEINBERG- DUISBURG		2.00
9th	00.30	HR 350	F/Lt GILLIATT	NAVIGATOR (25)	OPS Patrol of rail and road movement in area CLESFELD- RHEINE- MUNSTER- NIJMEN- HAMM- OSNABRUCK		3.00
9th	21.30	HR 350	F/Lt GILLIATT	NAVIGATOR (28)	OP Patrol of rail and road movement in area RIJKSEN ENSCHEDE BORKEN XANTEN		2.00
16th	14.30	HR 350	F/Lt GILLIATT	NAVIGATOR	N.F.T	.50	
17th	14.55	HR 350	F/Lt GILLIATT	NAVIGATOR	N.F.T.	.20	
21st	00.20	HR 350	F/Lt GILLIATT	NAVIGATOR (57)	OP Patrol of area ROERMOND VENLO along R.L. to from REES along RHINE to DUSSELDORF		2.00
31st	17.00	HR 350	F/Lt GILLIATT	NAVIGATOR	N.F.T. Photo junction flying	.50	

Total this ... 228.40 | 140.25

Time carried forward :—   119·40 144·25

Date	Hour	Aircraft Type and No.	Pilot	Duty	Remarks (including results of bombing, gunnery, exercises, etc.)	Flying Times Day	Night
FEB 1945 (cont)	11·15	Mosquito HR 156	F/Lt BILLIATT	NAVIGATOR ㉓	OPERATION CLARION. Day Op:- Patrol to attack all movement on rd. KIEL - NEUMÜNSTER. HAMBURG and rd. KIEL - NEUMÜNSTER. bombs from 5 mile S.S.W. NEUMÜNSTER. attacked - bombed and strafed line dropped. visibility 4m. Flak mod. Made to get experience	4·30	
3/2 th	23·30	PZ 241	F/Lt BILLIATT	NAVIGATOR ㉔	Op:- Patrol of area FLENSBURG - long Op on Areas HUSUM - FLENSBG. NEBEL. Bomber Patrols at SCHLESWIG		2·00
27 th	18·00	HR 207	F/Lt BILLIATT	NAVIGATOR ㉕	AIRCRAFT TEST.		
28 Feb 1945	02·10	PZ 241	F/Lt BILLIATT	NAVIGATOR ㉖	Op:- Patrol of railway junction at ITZEHOE. Attacked ITZEHOE area. NET ZERO loads brought back. 2 LOCOMOTIVES bombed and strafed. Many attacks on engines		2·40

Summary for FEB. 1945	(107 hrs.)	

	Day	Night
A/c MOSQUITO	4·30 3·00	14·25
Unit:- 107 Sqdn.		
Date:- 1st Mar. 1945		
Signature:- J. C. S/L c/o		

.... Flu..... of A. FLIGHT

.... W/Cdr. o/c 107 Sqdn.

Total Time ...... 125·55 146·05

Time carried forward — 23:15 | 145:05

Date	Hour	Aircraft Type and No.	Pilot	Duty	Remarks (including results of bombing, gunnery, exercises, etc.)	Flying Times Day	Night
MARCH 1945		MOSQUITO					
5th	01:25	PZ 241	F/Lt GILLIATT	NAVIGATOR (31)	Patrol of area East of Rhine between MOSBURG, MÖRSBERG. Bombs scattered, a road blocking 3 miles north of RATINGEN. N.F.T and search for intruding aircraft.	.40	1:55
6th	14:00	PZ 241	F/Lt GILLIATT	NAVIGATOR			
8/9th	01:30	PZ 241	F/Lt GILLIATT	NAVIGATOR (32)	Patrol of area KASSEL-MARBURG-PADERBORN. ABRILLEN USAA. Returned soon after reaching target area due to icing.		2:50
9th	18:45	PZ 241	F/Lt GILLIATT	NAVIGATOR (33)	Patrol of area MARBURG-NEUSTADT-KASSEL-HÜMME		3:05
11/12th	00:30	PZ 241	F/Lt GILLIATT	NAVIGATOR (34)	Patrol area OSNABRÜCK-HANNOVER. STENDAL. Attacked M/T and train 270°. APELDORN 5. N.F.T and fire to french firing pointer.	1:00	3:30
14th	13:15	HR 207	F/Lt GILLIATT	NAVIGATOR (35)			
14th	19:50	PZ 241	F/Lt GILLIATT	NAVIGATOR	Night patrol area HANAU-HERSFELD-EISENACH. Bombed and cannoned train at SCHLÜCHTERN junction.		2:50
16th	20:05	PZ 241	F/Lt GILLIATT	NAVIGATOR (36)	Night patrol area MEPPEL-GRONINGEN. Bombed railway at HEETZUID (HEERENVEEN?).		2:50
17th	12:40	HR 354	F/Lt GILLIATT	NAVIGATOR	Air to french firing pointer.	1:00	

Total Time 236:15 | 162:05

Date	Hour	Aircraft Type and No.	Pilot	Duty	Remarks (including results of bombing, gunnery, exercises, etc.)	Flying Times	
						Day	Night
March 1945		Mosquito					
19/l/1945	06·00	PZ 241	F/Lt Elliott	Navigator (39)	OP: Patrol of fuel and road movement in the area. HALT OLPE HASSLIAR NO RU EITOE		2·30
20	10·30	TR 111	F/Lt Elliott	Navigator	AIR to ENGINE firing.	1·05	
21 n.	19·30	PZ 241	F/Lt Elliott	Navigator (38)	OP: Patrol of area OLDE-RONSCHER, ISSALOEN HATTENBURE. Bombed + strafed 3 trains. On 2nd tr. NE. ASSENHAUSEN, other train in by-line. REHERHAUSEN		2·46
22 n.	20·15	PZ 241	F/Lt Elliott	Navigator (38)	OP: Strike nr RHEESFELD in support of Allied crossing		2·00
23/24 n.	21·15	NS 939	F/Lt Elliott	Navigator (40)	OP: Strike on ANHEIBECK N of the Rhine		1·50

SUMMARY FOR MARCH 1945. (107 Sqdn)		
	DAY	NIGHT
A/c. MOSQUITO	3·45	26·05
Unit. 107 Sqdn		

Sig. Pilot

Signature: 107 Sqn.

Total Time ... 211·20 191·10

Date	Hour	Aircraft Type and No.	Pilot	Duty	Remarks (including results of bombing, gunnery, exercises, etc.)	Flying Times Day	Night
APRIL 1945 10 th.	16.30	Mosquito PZ 341	F/Lt GILLIATT	NAVIGATOR	N.F.T.	·15	
10/11 th.	20.55	Pz 341	F/Lt GILLIATT	NAVIGATOR ⓝ	OP: Patrol of area SOLTAU-POREA RUTHNICK-BIEHDEN (CELLE Attacked light m/t FRIESRAE) abandoned immediate a/c activity		4·15
11 th.	15.30	Pz 341	F/Lt GILLIATT	NAVIGATOR	N.F.T.	·40	
14 th.	21.35	FB 376	F/Lt GILLIATT	NAVIGATOR ⓝ	OP: Patrol of area NETHERLANDS, FLENSMORE. STOKEL to MARNE Attacked small two m/t TURER 4.		4·05
18/19 th.	22.05	Pz 341	F/Lt GILLIATT	NAVIGATOR ⓝ	OP: Patrol of area BOITZENBURG HAREURG-FREIBURG-370 KRI. 10-KIRCHBARCHU WISMAR		4·00
20 th.	02.20	Pz 341	F/Lt GILLIATT	NAVIGATOR ⓝ	OP: Patrol of area BOITZENBURG WISMAR-MÜRITZ LAKE NEUBURG-PERLEBURG REHLAU BRUG. S/f PANU.		4·10
21 th.	22.30	Pz 341	F/Lt GILLIATT	NAVIGATOR	OP: Abortive Gee u/s after 45 mins out.		1·30
22 th.	15.00	NS 958	F/Lt GILLIATT	NAVIGATOR	Air to ground firing	1·00	
24 th.	22.00	Pz 341	F/Lt GILLIATT	NAVIGATOR ⓝ	OP: Rambes BREMEN under M.R.C.P. control. Patrol of area NEUHAUS WESTRAUNA FLENSBURG ECKERNFORDE.		4·05

Total Time ... 239·15 | 143 | ·15

Date	Hour	Aircraft Type and No.	Pilot	Duty	Remarks (including results of bombing, gunnery, exercises, etc.)	Flying Times Day	Night
APRIL 1945 (cont)	3.50	MOSQUITO $4×241$	F/Lt GILLITT	NAVIGATOR (40)	DV: Part of the WESTERLAND - FLENSBURG ... WAARI - along KIEL CANAL ALTENBRUCH		4.20

NO. 107 SQUADRON - BATTLE ORDER - NIGHT 26/27 APRIL 1945.

	AIRCRAFT	PILOT		NAVIGATOR		VHF NO.
A	RG 605	P/O	SAVAGE	P/O	FIELD	61
B	MG 953	F/Lt	LACEY	P/O	PARK	91
C	RB 530	P/O	BAGLEY	P/O	FISHER	66
D	TA 146	F/L	SMITH	P/O	PRATT	77
F	PZ 172	F/L	BENELAND	P/O	LACEY	68
G	TA 375	F/L	BADGETT	W/O	LEWIS	69
J	NS 853	Lt.	BUTTON	P/O	METLOW	62
Q	PZ 423	F/L	INGLEMAN	P/O	MOON	64
R	MR 354	P/L	CONKIE	P/O	NESBIT	93
S	PZ 576	W/O	MARSHALL	P/B	BEECH	60
T	PZ 336	F/L	McMILLAN	P/O	THORPE	92
V	HR 207	F/O	GRAINGER	P/S	HULL	67
W	PZ 241	F/L	GUILLATT	P/O	...	67

9HY

ORDERS ON BATTLE ORDER: 13
" " LEAVE: 5
" " REST: 3
" " NOT AVAILABLE: 2   24+

					R. VELREL (HIGH RORY) CROYDON		
						.35	
						3·00	

Eric Arnith
2.10.05

| 26th | 11·00 | F | F/O BRADSHAW | NAVIGATOR | Sea SONTRY. BASE MARSTRIGHT. BASE WAVER } Good weather for trip. | | 2·00 |

Au FLIGHT ROTLENE BASE

| 26th | 11·45 | F | F/Lt BRADSHAW | NAVIGATOR | VELREL - BASE | | ·50 |

| | | | | | | | 1·10 |

TOTAL TIME: 246·5 199·35

Badge and motto of RAF Squadron 107

Part 3:

Wartime Operational Service 1944-1945

Operational Squadron 107, Lasham, Hampshire.
    Motto: *Nous y serons*. (We will be there.)

Significant events of WW2
1944

- 22nd January: Allied landings in Anzio.
- 27th January: end of the siege of Leningrad.
- February: Allies bomb monastery at Monte Cassino.
- March: Hungary occupied by Germans.
- 10th April: Soviets capture Odessa.
- 12th May: Germans surrender in the Crimea.
- 25th May: Germans retreat from Anzio.
- 5th June: Allies enter Rome.
- 6th June: D-Day landings on the north coast of France (Operation Overlord/Neptune).
- 27th June: USA forces take Cherbourg.

- 3rd July: Soviets retake Minsk.
- 9th July: Allies take Caen.
- 20th July: assassination attempt on Adolf Hitler fails.
- 21st July: USA landings on Guam.
- 25th July: Allied break-out from Normandy begins (Operation Cobra).
- 15th August: Allied invasion of southern France begins (Operation Dragoon).
- 25th August: Allies liberate Paris.
- 30th August: Germans abandon Bulgaria.
- 31st August: Soviets capture Bucharest.
- 22nd September: Boulogne liberated.
- 26th September: Estonia occupied by Soviets.
- 28th September: Calais liberated.
- 15th October: Athens liberated. General Rommel commits suicide.
- 20th October: Belgrade liberated.
- 23rd October: Soviets enter East Prussia.
- 4th November: surrender of Axis forces.
- 16th December: German attack through the Ardennes – Battle of the Bulge – begins.

We were posted to Lasham on the 16th Sept 1944, a date indelibly etched on my memory.

On the way we met an officer already based there, who'd been recalled from leave. This was our first suspicion that something big was on the cards. On arrival, the Squadron CO explained to us that an important operation was planned for the next day. So far, he had no further information, but

WE DID WHAT WE HAD TO

he'd recalled all his experienced crews who were on leave. If it turned out that any of them couldn't get back in time, then we would have to go…

He told us to head down to dispersal, get an aircraft and go for a flight so that we could become totally conversant with the area.

This was it.

We were also ordered to attend briefing next morning, at which we were shown a model of the German army barracks at Arnhem, though at the time we weren't told it was Arnhem. Twelve aircraft from 107 Squadron were to go in by daylight, one hour before the airborne forces landed there, and attack the barracks. Definitely dicey.

There were four of us, two new sprog crews, who'd just arrived – we already knew the other two men from training.

Immediately after the briefing, a serious-looking CO comes to tell us that one of the recalled experienced crews had not made it back from leave: one of us would have to go on the op.

He tossed a coin.

Court called heads and it came down *tails*. That's it, I thought. We've lost, so we go. But, no. That wasn't how it worked. "Congratulations!" said the CO to the other team. "You've won the toss, so you're going." That was the spirit of the squadron: not exactly gung-ho death or glory, but definitely to do with honour, rather an old-fashioned word nowadays.

At Lasham I was now part of what was called a *wing*, made up of three squadrons: mine, which was 107, a pre-war squadron with a proud record: 613 Squadron, which was almost entirely British: and 305, a Polish squadron, which had all sorts of nationalities to make up the crew as they were running out of men. The Poles couldn't see why we didn't fly in all weathers – they were raring to go. Their country had been invaded, after all, and I thought I could understand their mentality.

Out of my squadron, all the navigators were British, except one. There were a few British pilots, two or three New Zealanders, several Aussies, quite a few Canadians, including Court, an American, a Dutchman, a Norwegian and a South African Major. We were a cosmopolitan lot and if there was ever an impromptu party in the mess, which was quite often, it was always 107 who started it!

After the coin toss, Dave, the navigator of the other crew, got the collywobbles. Understandably. Your first op is pretty terrifying, especially a daylight mission, flying at low level. You know that you're going to lose one or two aircraft. I did Dave's flight plan for him and went out to see them off with a strange mix of feelings – relief being uppermost, I must confess. It was a Sunday, but on operational airfields there were no church parades. However, they were relaying a radio service on loudspeakers. As Dave and Doug climbed into their aircraft, the congregation began singing *Nearer my God to thee*, not the most appropriate hymn in the circumstances. *Onward Christian Soldiers* would have been a better choice, I thought grimly.

I hung around the airfield all day, waiting for the returning planes. I was very on edge. It could have been me out there. The Battle of Arnhem, part of Monty's plan to gain access to the Ruhr, turned into a disaster for the

Allies, as has been shown since in the textbooks and the many films made. Doug and Dave came back safely from their first sortie, but we lost two planes that day.

My first op was the following Saturday, 23rd September, 1944.

It was a night flight and we were due to fly over the Dutch coast, just south of Rotterdam, after going low over the Channel at only 50 ft., which was dicey in the dark. Then we were to cruise at the height of 4,000 ft, basically too low for the heavy Ack-Ack guns, and too high for the ground artillery. I told Court that in a minute's time we'd be over the Dutch coast and in exactly one minute, by pure coincidence, the coastal defence searchlights came on, coning us. It felt like a welcome of sorts, but we were highly visible.

My log book tells me that we patrolled Venlo, Roermund, Cologne and Dusseldorf that night, but I can remember more about our return to base than the op, itself, which must have gone pretty smoothly.

On our return, we were diverted to Dunsford base, near Guildford, because a plane had crash landed on our runway. Returning to Lasham, first thing next day, we came into land at 135mph – you have to land a Mossie at extra speed – and hit the concrete runway with a hell of a noise. The undercarriage had collapsed. Exercises back in Canada had trained me well: I released the escape hatch, unplugged my harness and radio transmitter and switched off the petrol, in case the plane caught fire. I'd evacuated the plane, before it came to a stop, and legged it across the runway. The plane didn't catch fire and Court was left shouting and swearing at the debacle. Though it may have made a funny story in the Mess later, both of us were shaken up by the incident and what seemed like an inauspicious start to our tour of operations. (*see footnote at end of chapter*)

Once inside the station, we looked up at the chalked ops board, like they do in the films. In our squadron, 50 ops made a tour, though in some squadrons it was less. On the board it said *Fl. Lt Gilliatt, Flying Officer Hill: Ops completed 1. Ops remaining: 49.* At that moment, I didn't feel I was a very good candidate for life insurance.

We were grounded, pending a brief enquiry, which found that an airlock in the mechanics had caused the failure of the undercarriage to retract.

While grounded, I met one officer who loved ops and regarded each one as a challenge; a highly decorated pilot, he'd done three tours, mainly in daylight. He'd been shot up and wounded several times. He'd flown Blenheims, Bostons, Mossies, and other aircraft, too. He'd been permanently grounded, but was desperate to fly.

"You're Gilliatt's navigator, aren't you?" he hailed me one evening. "How would you like to fly with me?" Rather in awe of this super-hero, I felt I had to agree. Off he went to get permission. To my relief they wouldn't let him. Thank God! The view was that he was a danger, over-confident and bomb-happy. It happened. The adrenalin-rush became addictive for some men.

Most of us were less complacent. When you fly low-level *intruder* operations at one thousand feet into a target area, you learn on the job. You gain experience and you learn to be cautious, not a dare-devil, because you can be more effective that way. For example, on our fourth or fifth op, we'd been to the briefing, done all the work for it, done the test flight. It was the early hours when the plan completely changed. A report had come in that the German army was evacuating Holland and we were to go and attack one of their ships. I had to do a very hasty flight plan. The adrenalin kicked in as we flew over and spotted the ship we were to sink. But we made the mistake of attacking from the sea, not the land. As we're diving in, the ship is firing at us and as we're pulling out, at our most vulnerable, the shore guns are firing at us. What we should have done was to circle around, attack from shore side and then pull out over the sea. If you survive, you don't make the same mistake twice.

* * *

107 Squadron was involved in what were called *intruder* missions, flying Mosquitos in relays to upset the enemy and attack them when they were least expecting it. Most of the time, you took off late afternoon to early evening and flew on your own in the darkness over Germany or Occupied Europe, doing a patrol along specific flight paths. You were looking out for ways to be a nuisance to the enemy in every way possible, spotting buildings showing a light, making precision attacks on enemy aircraft in their airspace and bombing secondary targets like railways, roads and ports, as well as primary targets like military bases.

There was also a mental war being waged by these tactical aircraft. Because of their speed (up to 388mph) and the frequency of the patrols, the Mossies were a heavy presence. In addition to their ubiquity, they were also extremely stealthy, so had a surprise element which led to a specific German word being coined: *Mosquitopanik*. This summed up just how threatening the plane could be, how it engendered a very real fear because of its precision attacks. I once dropped flares, lighting up a Mossie just below me which I didn't even realise was there. The crew of the other plane were not amused. Goering, himself, was very envious of the Allies' advantage in having designed such an effective small, two-man plane, as the following quotation shows: *In 1940 I could at least fly as far as Glasgow in most of my aircraft, but not now! It makes me furious when I see the Mosquito. I turn green and yellow with envy. The British, who can afford aluminium better than we can, knock together a beautiful wooden aircraft that every piano factory over there is building, and they give it a speed which they have now increased yet again. What do you make of that? There is nothing the British do not have. They have the geniuses and we have the nincompoops. After the war is over I'm going to buy a British radio set – then at least I'll own something that has always worked.***

Because of their size, you were tightly strapped in so you could hardly move. There was no shelf or desk so I put my parachute on my knees and used this as a ledge for charts, pencil etc. You were working all the time but there were lots of times when you didn't know where you were going till you got over the sea which showed up in the moonlight. The two of you were alone in the darkness. Sometimes it was by *guess or by God*. But you didn't want to call for a homing signal to help you, partly from pride and partly for your own safety in case you were intercepted.

On 105 Squadron, when you'd completed four or five ops, you were allocated your own aircraft for all future flights. Thus we did 24 ops in Aircraft HR350 and the remainder in PL241.

The plane doesn't just belong to the pilot and navigator, but to the ground crew as well. They're vital. They're responsible for all the checks, repairs and maintenance and aircrew depend on them for their safety. They're the guys who literally pick up the pieces after an op when the Mosquito returns damaged or missing bits, and somehow they have to make it ready for the next sortie as soon as possible. Before an op, you do a short test flight to make sure everything is ok. As navigator, I wasn't really needed on this, so I used to ask the ground crew if they'd like to go up – it was often their only chance to fly in the Mosquito they looked after.

A bond of trust and mutual respect soon developed between us and our ground crew. As an example, on *Operation Clarion*, a daylight raid with greater potential for losses, Court and I had climbed into the cockpit and were ready to shut the door. As we waited for the step ladder we used to be taken away, one of the ground crew, a very tall Cockney, inevitably known as Lofty, said to me quietly, "Please come back, sir."

* * *

Xmas 1944 was a very different kind of Xmas.

On the 3rd November 1944, we'd been moved to Epinoy, a mile or so north of Cambrai in Northern France, to an operational airfield vacated by the Luftwaffe.

Everyone was looking forward to a good Xmas in RAF style with our squadron tradition that the officers serve the other ranks at Xmas dinner. We also knew that the Entertainments officer had booked a band from Brussels.

However, General von Rundstedt had other ideas and deliberately planned his counter-attack on the Ardennes over Xmas so the Allies would have limited or no air support due to poor weather. He'd made significant advances which was distinctly frightening. This put paid to all the organised festivities, not to mention the chance for everyone to unwind and release some of the tension which inevitably builds up with regular ops.

It was very foggy. The whole squadron made ready to fly if the fog lifted. Eventually it did, but only four planes had taken off for night-flying tests (NFTs) before the fog came down again and closed in. The four planes were diverted back to an English base and stuck there for Xmas. The rest of us didn't take off that night, but from Xmas Eve 1944, when the cloud lifted, to New Year's Eve, came a whole succession of ops. I did seven altogether. For example, as my log book states for New Year's Day: *patrol of enemy positions in breakthrough 'bulge' in vicinity of St Vith...* On the 6th January, I recorded the following: *strike on reported enemy movement of M/T by ferry at Gorinchem. Moderate light flak encountered.*

Von Rundstedt's offensive was failing, and due to the Allies' airpower, Hitler gave up the whole enterprise; by the end of January 1945, the German armies were back where they started, the narrow salient gained then lost.

After the intensive series of ops, our Entertainments

Officer booked a local band to compensate for our missed Xmas. They turned out to be dreadful! Wing Commander Laddie Lucas, a highly decorated pilot, decided that the only way to get them off the stage was to get them drunk. So we did. That was fun.

Significant events of WW2
1945

- 1st January: Germans withdraw from the Ardennes.
- 17th January: Soviets capture Warsaw.
- 26th January: Japanese retreat to Chinese coast and Soviets liberate Auschwitz.
- 4th-11th February: Yalta Conference with the *Big Three* – Roosevelt, Churchill and Stalin.
- The Soviet Union has control of Eastern Europe.
- 19th February: USA landings on Iwo Jima.
- 1st April: USA troops encircle the Ruhr.
- 12th April: Allies liberate Buchenwald and Belsen concentration camps. Roosevelt dies and Truman becomes president.
- 8th May: VE Day in Europe. Germany surrenders to the Red Army in Berlin.
- July: Potsdam Conference. Germany is officially sectioned into 4 zones of occupation.
- 6th August: USA drops 13 kiloton atomic bomb (Little Boy) on Hiroshima, which kills 80,000 people.
- 8th August: Russia declares war on Japan.
- 9th August: USA drops 22 kiloton atomic bomb *(Fat Man)* on Nagasaki, killing 70,000.

- 14th August: the Japanese surrender.
- 15th August: Japanese Emperor gives surrender broadcast – VJ Day.
- 2nd September: World War 2 ends.

In February 1945 came *Operation Clarion*, a propaganda op, and the only daylight one I flew.

The plan was that at a certain hour of a certain morning – namely the 22nd February – 20,000 RAF and USAF bombers and escort fighter planes were to be flying in designated areas over the airbases, autobahns and railways, of Germany. This was to demonstrate our strength in the air, and, it was hoped, to accelerate the end of the war. For the first and only time we were given free rein to bomb anything – hitherto we'd always been given specific orders and targets. We flew in tight formation, in lines of four. We were number 3 in the leading line. Then, when we reached Germany, we split into twos and, as the more experienced crew, we took the lead in our pair. In our appointed area, we flew in low level to attack a train, did what we had to do, then climbed away, out over the countryside. Everything was mapped out below us, clearly visible. We could even watch a single farm vehicle, making its way along a track: the tractor was pulling a cartload of manure. I can still see the farmer's face to this day, as he looked up in fear. He saw the Mossie coming in low and dived headfirst into the manure. It would have been funny if it hadn't been war. It was still quite funny. I suggested to Court that we leave him alone – he'd got enough to deal with, we decided.

We realised we couldn't go back the way we'd come,

because the Luftwaffe would be waiting, so we flew off in a different direction, crossing the Kiel Canal at one thousand feet. It was heavily fortified and we could see several U-boats, like models on the water, which didn't seem to be moving. I remember it was a beautiful day, unbelievably beautiful. The sun shone up there in the *footless halls of air*, to quote from the poem at the end of Section 3. We came out over the sea, as low as we could to avoid the radar, and got home safely by flying low level all the way.

Back at debriefing we were asked about the Kiel Canal. "Fine," we said.

"No, it b..... well wasn't," interrupted the other Mossie crew. "The Ack-Ack was coming up behind you, in front of us, around us, everywhere... You were completely unaware!"

The only fire we'd encountered came from a British Destroyer which turned its guns on us, not a new experience. I've been fired on by German air and land forces, but also by the British Army and the Royal Navy. Talk about friendly fire – it's anything but friendly! But it's the automatic response. In the Mosquito I was equipped with a Very pistol to send off flares of different colours so you could identify yourself with the colour of the day. The red flare was, of course, the distress signal and I always kept a red cartridge in the gun to let off in case of friendly fire. Nine times out of ten, it worked and the firing stopped as soon as they realised it was one of their own planes.

The next big op was the night the Allies crossed the Rhine, which, as at El Alamein, would inevitably take place in *Monty's Moonlight* – the artificial illumination provided by the 344 searchlight unit for night operations. This would mean that we would be instantly visible if any enemy aircraft were in the area and I would need to keep a constant look-out when we reached our target. We did two flights in support, with the new aid, MRCP (Mobile Radar Control Post), which told us where and when the army needed assistance. We were sent to Cologne, ordered to fly at ten thousand feet, a height we'd never flown before. As we reached the designated point, we were immediately taken over by the radar on the ground. It told us which course to fly, when to open the bomb bay, when to drop the bombs. All controlled. When we got back to base, we were told to refuel, re-arm, and go up again.

As it happened, I went on leave the next day – we got a week's leave every seven weeks. They always flew us back in a Dakota to Northolt or Croydon, which meant I could pop home for a short while. When I reached West Ruislip tube station, there were the news-stands selling the evening papers with large headlines blazoned on them: *Monty crosses the Rhine!*

I was there last night, I thought to myself. I was up there in the skies, looking down on the Rhine... It seemed surreal.

* * *

The last battle order for 107 squadron was given on the 26th April, 1945. I've pasted a copy in my log book. For our last op, Court and I did another patrol of the Kiel Canal.

I can honestly say, at this stage, that I never felt nervous before going on one of our operational flights, even after the briefing, when you had received information about adverse

WE DID WHAT WE HAD TO

weather conditions and the details relating to your target area. You had to block out worries which could affect your concentration on your flight duties. Anxiety could grow and grow, as it did with some men, till you became a bag of nerves. One crew got into a terrible state and on one flight left the radio on so that they were recorded at base. Understandably, they were grounded. If you could help it, you didn't want to be grounded because of the stigma attached to this, of being charged with LMF. *Low moral fibre.*

It may seem incredible but, as I climbed into the aircraft for an operational flight, I never thought that it might be my last one.

* * *

The German document of surrender was signed on the 7th May 1945 and the VE Day celebrations broke out, not surprisingly, on the following day. Adolf Hitler had committed suicide in his Berlin bunker on the 30th April.

A short while later, we had a visit from Air Vice Marshall Sir Basil Embry, Air Officer Commanding 2 Group 2nd Tactical Airforce, of which we were part. He'd also been the CO of 107 at the start of the war. He'd been shot down in the evacuation of Dunkirk and taken prisoner. Then he'd made a famous and daring escape which involved throttling three guards, but on his return was forbidden to fly because there was a price on his head. Being the man he was, he had his own aircraft and, if there was a dangerous raid, he went, under his own steam, as it were, though he was never allowed to lead the attack.

If any of the non-commissioned aircrew were recommended for a commission they'd go to HQ to be interviewed by Sir Basil. "*What's he like? Got any hints?*" they'd ask. We'd tell them to be prepared. He'd always glare at you and bark out: "Do you hate the Hun?"

If you said yes, instantly, you'd get a commission!

If you hesitated, you were stuffed. No commission. That was his mentality.

Anyway, as mentioned above, at the end of the war, he came down to our wing and ordered the squadrons to assemble. He addressed us all – *wonderful job you've done* etc. He expected we were all looking forward to demob and to seeing our loved ones… etc. etc. We began to think he was human after all. Then he drew himself up to his full height of 5 2" and shouted, "And if I had my way, I'd have the whole bloody lot of you in the Far East tomorrow!"

Thank you, sir.

*From *Mosquito at War* by Chaz Bower, chapter '*Canadian Capers*' by John Conlin.

After taking off from his diversion point, a short distance from Lasham, Gilliat found the undercart would not come up and immediately jumped to the conclusion that the ground crew on the diversion field had neglected to take off the locking nuts. Since it wasn't too far he decided to fly over with the wheels down, but he neglected to select down again before landing and subsequent enquiry revealed that the failure to retract had been caused by an airlock in the hydraulic system.

** (https://en.wikiquote.org/wiki/Talk:Hermann_G%C3%B6ring)

Part 4:

Post-war Service 1945-1946

A tour of ops in 107 Squadron was 50. After that you could be grounded, and become an instructor, or you could sign up to do a second tour of 30. As the war was drawing to a close, a lot of men were doing this. Court and I had flown 46 operations when the war finally ended.

Suddenly you could make plans again, your life no longer on hold. It felt strange to re-focus, to think of yourself and your loved ones. What to do next?

Betty wanted us to get married. But in the endgame of the war, it was still uncertain when exactly it would all be over. I decided to apply for a second tour and for a month's leave, to which I was entitled, to get married. Though with all the protracted uncertainty, I still wasn't sure whether I'd be able to attend my own wedding. I got lucky again and the end of war coincided with my leave.

There wasn't much time to organise the wedding, but Betty's parents got on with it, as you did in those days.

Our wedding on the 26th May 1945 at St Saviour's Church, Alexandra Palace, London, with bridesmaid, Joan Miller, and Best Man, Peter Hill.

I wanted my close friends from the RAF, and, of course, Court, to come, but didn't know if they'd all be able to make it. As it turned out they all did, every last one. Wearing their best blues, of course. My in-laws were besieged with calls – I still remember their North London phone number which was *Enterprise 3109* – saying, "we've landed, how do we get to Alexandra Palace?"

As my brother and I arrived at the church, one of my mates handed me a huge bottle of champagne, the real stuff. "I can't walk into the church carrying that!" I said. At the reception Betty's parents had organised a pianist but by the time *my wife and I* were ready to go off on honeymoon Arthur Liddell, a very good pianist from 107 Squadron, had commandeered the piano. Thank God we were leaving.

At the tube station, another pilot I knew tipped me off

Court Gilliatt, 1997.

to the effect that my pals were trying to find out where I was staying. We made ourselves scarce, checking all the way to the hotel that we weren't being followed. Very Harry Lime.

On honeymoon I started having serious doubts about what I'd done. Regarding my career, not my marriage, I hasten to add. They could send me to the Far East, where hostilities continued. Perhaps my war wasn't over. Incidentally, when they had eventually put some Mossies into Burma, they'd found that the heat melted the glue holding the wooden aircraft together. So I wouldn't be flying Mosquitoes.

I didn't see Court again until several years later. When I got back to 107 Squadron after the end of my leave, all the Canadian pilots had been repatriated.

Court had always wanted to do a university degree. He

(including results of bombing

**COURTNEY (COURT)
SHIPPEY SPURR
GILLIATT**
BRIGADIER GENERAL (RET'D),
CANADIAN ARMED FORCES, DFC

Born 1921 in Annapolis Royal, NS, Court died Oct. 17, 2008 at the Queensway Carleton Hospital, Ottawa. He died as he lived - a gentle man and a gentleman.

Survived by his sister Hortense Marie (Sally) Padmore of Toronto, and his wife of 60 years, Helen (Edwards), daughter Vicki (Paul Hand), son Chris (Angie Wong), daughter Cathy (David Walker) and grandchildren Michael, Peter and Robin Hand, Richard and Anna Gilliatt, Christopher, Matt and Alex Walker.

Before the war, Courtney attended the Nova Scotia Agricultural College (NSAC) where he won the Governor General Medal and the Macdonald Scholarship (1941). In his wartime service he was a pilot with the 107th RAF Squadron, flying Mosquitos over Germany and France with this RAF navigator Johnnie Hill. Courtney was awarded the Distinguished Flying Cross for his service.

After the war, he attended McGill University (Macdonald Campus) and graduated in 1947 with his B.Sc. He reenlisted in the service after graduation.

He served at Randolph Air Force Base TX, and Scott Air Force Base IL, and then Portage la Prairie MB, as commanding officer of the flight training school. After time in Trenton and Winnipeg, two tours in Europe followed - Ramstein, Germany (4rth ATAF) and four years as the senior Canadian officer at SHAPE in Mons, Belgium. Back in Ottawa, Courtney enjoyed the position as one of the honorary aides to Governors Vanier and Mitchener.

In 1993, he was honoured with the Distinguished Alumnus Award by NSAC for his broad life achievements. After retiring from the Canadian Armed Forces in 1976, Courtney earned an M.A. degree in International Affairs at Carleton University (1977).

Courtney's life was not all work. He had a great affection and affinity for the natural world, especially birds. Peterson's Field Guides to birds and flowers were an important part of Gilliatt countryside travels. His love of nature and reading had been sparked at an early age by his mother and father, Hortense and Frederick Gilliatt. His sister's interest in reading led her to become a career librarian. Courtney's reading joys in retirement centred on serious political and historical literature. This good family man will be missed.

A remembrance service will be held at the Central Chapel of Hulse, Playfair and McGarry, 315 McLeod Street, Ottawa on Saturday, November 8 at 11:00 hours. In lieu of flowers, please remember your local Food Bank.

p.s. Before his death, Courtney managed to complete his vote at the advance poll in the recent federal election. A true Canadian.

*Condolences/Donations/Tributes
at: mcgarryfamily.ca
613-233-1143*

was very fond of botany and, growing up in Nova Scotia, often used to go into the woods alone at weekends and live off the land. He was an expert on fungi. On his return from active service, he went to McGill University and took a degree, supported by the Canadian government. Then he re-enlisted In the Royal Canadian Air Force. Later the air force amalgamated with the army, as it did in the States, and Court had a very distinguished career, eventually achieving the rank of Brigadier General.

Court and Helen Gilliatt's gravestone in the National Military Cemetery of Canada, Ottawa.

He made contact soon after the war and later he and his wife, Helen, came over to England to stay with us, and I went to Ottawa to see him. He met my parents, too, having left a kitbag of clothes with them until the end of the war. We continued to keep in touch and visit each other until his death in 2008. His obituary read: *he died as he had lived, a gentle man and a gentleman.* I'm still in touch with his wife, Helen, and met his son during my visit to Ottawa in 2002.

He sent me a book written by a Canadian navigator about the part played by Mosquitoes in WW2, having asked the author to sign it. His own dedication ran as follows: *To Johnny Hill, my navigator on 107 Squadron. An excellent navigator and faithful friend.*

* * *

If you think returning to the squadron after the war was a bit of an anti-climax, you're right. Why had I signed on again? I was very bored. 107 Squadron continued to serve as part of the British Air Forces of Occupation (BAFO) after the war. It was disbanded in 1948 and re-numbered as No. 11 RAF Squadron. I left 107 Squadron in August 1945 and joined BAFO at Buckeburg, near Maden, Germany, where flying mainly consisted of taking VIPs around. Then I got the opportunity in October of the same year to go to British Air Command, Berlin, so I transferred to Gatow, Goering's equivalent of Cranwell.

My duties there were the same as at Buckeburg – navigating flights in Ansons, modified for passenger use, for service personnel and VIPs to destinations in England and western Europe. One such flight deserves a mention. We were flying the General Officer in charge of commanding British Forces, Berlin, together with his entourage, to England. We heard a knocking noise in the cockpit which grew louder and louder till it sounded like machine gun fire. We tested all the controls. No success. A knock on the cockpit door and there stood the General's ADC, spluttering and demanding to know whether everything was OK. "We're working on the problem," we assured him. Subtext: *we'll have to make a forced landing if it continues.*

Then I happened to look at the window ledge where I usually kept my long Perspex ruler. Ansons, being pretty old, are not streamlined and, with the tilt of the plane to the rear, it had slipped down between the windowpane and the main fuselage. Caught in the slipstream of the starboard engine, it was flapping violently against the fuselage, making the aforesaid deafening noise. Relief! I pulled it in and went off to tell the general we'd *resolved* the problem. I didn't explain the cause.

I was very lucky to complete my RAF career at Gatow, which was a lovely station set in natural surroundings. Situated a short distance from the western boundary of the city, it had not suffered bomb damage. Life there was interesting and exciting. Berlin was well within the Russian occupation area but at the end of the war the Western Allies had requested a presence there, so the city was divided into four sectors, French, British, American and Russian. The Russians, being hostile, had imposed restricted access from the west by means of the 5-mile corridor, south-west to Frankfurt, due west to Magdeburg and north-west to Hamburg. You strayed from these corridors at your peril. A year or so after I left Berlin, the Russians, in an attempt to remove the Western presence there and take control, stopped all ground movement in the corridors – their blockade of Berlin, one of the first escalations in the Cold War. They hadn't, however, foreseen the RAF response to this in the shape of the huge humanitarian effort of the *Berlin Airlift*.

We had lots of visits from VIPs and celebrities to see the terrible damage suffered by Berlin during the war. On one occasion I was part of a crew that took Sir Walter Citreen, of TUC fame, for a flight around the city and another time our passenger was Mabel Strickland, the then renowned editor of *The Times* of Malta. Among the celebrities who came to entertain us, and whom I met afterwards in the Mess, were Evelyn Laye, Geraldo and Leslie Sarony. I shall never forget the visit of Fl/Lt Arthur Wint, the famous West Indian athlete, an 880yd world champion, who competed in the 1948 Olympic Games. When he came into our dining room, the German waitresses completely froze! After years of racial indoctrination, they couldn't believe that a black man was an RAF officer, and they had to be ordered to serve him.

After the war cigarettes had become currency in Berlin for a while. One cigarette equalled ten Deutschmarks. Children used to search for stubs on the ground. It was terrible to see this and watch humans degraded in this way.

The Danish economy had recovered quickly after the war and part of my flying duties involved frequent trips to Copenhagen, where Mosquitoes had carried out a daylight raid on the Gestapo HQ. One aircraft flying too low had hit a chimney stack and caused civilian deaths, so we had an air display to raise money for the dependants and the Mossies were represented in a formation of seven. There's a photo in my log book and a caption which tells me that I was in the last plane.

Unlike Spitfires and Hurricanes, Mosquitoes have a limited performance in air shows. I can't recall now the name of the pilot who led the formation, but, I believe, he led the Mosquito daylight *Letterbox* bombing raid on

Copenhagen, 1945

Mosquito formation over Kastrup airport, Copenhagen, 1st July, 1945, with John's plane circled.

Gestapo HQ in The Hague. He came up with the idea that it would be impressive, visually, if the last plane touched down as he, in the first, reached the end of the runway. This would be very testing, not to mention risky, for my pilot, F/Lt Bradshaw, a Canadian; to make matters worse, we would be approaching the runway at Kastrup over the sea, between Malmo, Sweden, and the Danish coast. There would be turbulence during our descent, in addition to that caused by the slipstream of the plane in front of us.

But we did it!

The strange thing was that, after all the night flying, I didn't like seeing the ground as we came into land on daylight flights!

We felt proud when we read in the newspaper the next day that a quarter of the Danish population was estimated to have attended the show. And we received an invitation we couldn't refuse while we were in the air, returning to base. The Danish Resistance Organisation requested that the Mosquito crews remain as their guests for dinner at a top hotel in Copenhagen, with overnight accommodation arranged. It was an evening to remember.

We made many friends in Copenhagen, especially amongst the former Resistance members, and were given all sorts of food parcels, containing luxuries like butter, to take on flights to the UK, where food was still strictly rationed.

* * *

The time came for me to say farewell to the RAF.

I had done a total of 123.40 hours of night flying on

operations, with 4.20 daylight hours. Giving a total of 128 hours.

I had also completed 56.20 non-operational flying hours in the RAF, giving a grand total of 184.20 hours up to December 1945.

On August 10th 1946, from a base at Hamburg, I wrote in my log: *Farewell! Now on way home for demob*. While on the boat home, I heard that my old Squadron Leader, Wing Commander Paddy Maher, had been killed in a Mossie prang over the North German island of Sylt. He, it was, who'd written succinctly in my records at the end of the war: *Did a good job on operations with 107 Squadron*.

I was mentioned in despatches on 1st January, 1946. In October 1945 Court had been awarded the DFC (Distinguished Flying Cross, 3rd highest medal for RAF personnel).

* * *

I would like to end this section by including the poem, *High Flight*, in memory of all RAF Aircrew who were not so lucky as me. The poem was written in September 1941 by 19-year-old Pilot Officer, John Magee, an American in the Canadian Royal Air Force, while he was stationed at RAF Digby, Lincolnshire. It seems that he foresaw the future, as he was killed three months later when his aircraft collided with one flying from nearby Cranwell.

Oh, I have slipped the surly bonds of earth
And danced the skies on laughter-silvered wings;
Sunward I've climbed and joined
the tumbling mirth
Of sun-split clouds – and done a hundred things
You have not dreamed of –
wheeled and soared and swung
High into the sunlit silence. Hovering there
I've chased the shouting wind along and flung
My eager craft through footless halls of air.
Up, up the long delirious, burning blue
I've topped the wind – swept heights with easy grace,
Where never lark, or even eagle, flew;
And, while with silent, lifting mind I've trod
The high untrespassed sanctity of space,
Put out my hand and touched the face of God.

Part 5:

Post-War Career 1946–1982

When I was demobbed from the RAF in 1946, I returned to my pre-war employment with the Air Ministry, but now in the Accounts' department. I soon realised that my Civil Service salary would be a lot less than my pay as an RAF Flight Lieutenant, so, as I was now married, I decided that I needed to improve my future financial prospects. I studied for and passed the examination for Officers of Her Majesty's Customs and Excise. This grade was equivalent to that of Civil Service Higher Executive Officer, a bit higher up the chain from the familiar uniformed customs officer you encounter at ports and airports.

So in 1948 I joined Customs and Excise, and, as the following paragraphs illustrate, I ended up having five different careers within the same organisation. All were challenging but extremely interesting, so that when I retired in 1982 I could honestly say that I had had job satisfaction.

I started with an extensive training course which covered both the theory and practical aspects of Customs and Excise duties. I then become an unattached officer filling in for fixed station officers on annual or sick leave, before being assigned to London Central Collection, which covered all the excise stations in the city of London and along the North Thames Coastal Area as far east as Southend-on-Sea. In due course I obtained a fixed officer position in the City area which meant that I always covered the same offices – two at Whitbread Brewery in Chiswell Street near Moorgate, two at the Ardath Tobacco Company near Finsbury Square, and two separate excise stations located in the City area.

One memorable enquiry during the U/O period was a visit I had to make to the Shell HQ in the City. It concerned the re-importation of one of their foreign manufactured aircraft. I was taken to their Aircraft Division, and you can imagine my delight when I was introduced to the head of that organisation – the legendary WW2 fighter pilot ace – Douglas Bader.

In 1952 I secured my first fixed station position: one of three officers at Johnny Walkers' bonded warehouse in Commercial Road, Stepney. The work there was mainly practical since we controlled most of the vatting and bottling operations for delivery within the bond. We had to determine the contents and strengths of all the casks of whisky received, as well as checking all the bottle contents and strengths, since the various export markets all had different vat strengths and case contents. This may sound a rather fortuitous choice of company, especially where presents and free samples were concerned, but it did involve a lot of travelling. I was living with my family in

WE DID WHAT WE HAD TO

South Harrow, my second daughter having been born in the September of 1952, and needed to make the lengthy journey each day to Aldgate East. When it was my turn to open up the Revenue Lock, I had to be there before 8.30 am. So, eventually, in 1958, I managed to transfer to one of the Ealing excise stations much nearer home.

At Ealing it was like starting a completely new job, entailing more, in fact almost all, aspects of excise work. For instance, my main traders for import and export matters were H. J. Heinz and McVitie & Price. In those days there was an entertainment duty, too, so I also had to deal with five cinemas – two each for Ealing and Wembley, and one for Park Royal. I also had to visit the Park Royal greyhound track to check that all the bookmakers had the required Excise Licence, and to note the Tote betting figures.

Once a week, for example, I would visit the Guinness brewery to audit the beer duty accounts, and as a complete contrast, would also act for the Principal Probate Registry in Bush House, London, to process probate applications for small estates. The latter duty took up a lot of my time, especially during the winter months, but it was extremely interesting and rewarding, with the satisfaction that you were providing a worthwhile service for the public. The fee we charged, in those days, was £2 and 10 shillings. (£2.50). The advantage to being in an excise station, compared with the Stepney post, was that you could plan your day as you wished and were not tied to time attendance.

In 1966, when there was a large scale reorganisation of the department, I took the opportunity to transfer out of the London area, and was appointed to Southend Airport.

The family and I moved to the house in Leigh-on-Sea which is still my home today. My role at Southend Airport was Landing and Shipping Officer in the Customs Section. In the mid-sixties, the airport was extremely busy, second only to Heathrow regarding the volume of freight imported. The two mainline airlines based there were British Air Ferries, using Carvair Aircraft (converted DC4 planes), and Channel Airways who flew Propjet Viscounts. The former transported vehicles and freight to and from destinations in Europe, while the latter carried some freight, but mainly flew all the passengers on the foreign package holidays which were becoming extremely popular, part of the emerging post-war tourist industry. Once again I was in a time attendance post and was often required to work paid overtime. As most of the flying schedules ran late into the evenings and also at weekends, you never knew from one day to another when you would finish.

For example, on one weekend I remember starting at 9am on the Saturday and finishing at 3am the next morning, then being back on duty at 2pm the same day with another long shift. The plus side of all this was that by the time I left Southend Airport to work elsewhere, I had paid off my mortgage! Another plus was that I often came into contact with well-known people, such as the then Prime Minister, Edward Heath, the Archbishop of Canterbury, Prince Rainier of Monaco, and the famous racing driver, Graham Hill.

Another bonus was encountering a variety of weird and wonderful importations: for example, late one Friday afternoon, shortly after a scheduled Channel Airways flight from Jersey had landed, I was called to the counter by the Airline Cargo Manager and handed a customs entry for the importation of a live bear! To add to the drama, the bear was booked on an internal feeder (sic) aircraft which was due to depart 30 minutes later. Immediately, alarm bells start ringing in my head. What on earth were the rules for bears? I knew there were restrictions on the importation of dogs, so there had to be some similar regulations. I decided to phone the Animal Health Department at the Ministry of Agriculture and Fisheries for advice, but was told I couldn't get an answer until Monday morning, a typical Civil Service rebuff.

"I am sorry madam," I said, "but I need a decision now because the bear has got a plane to catch shortly and at this moment, I can tell you, he looks very angry indeed."

Eventually I was told that I could allow clearance provided I received a written undertaking from the agent that the necessary health documents would be lodged within the next forty-eight hours. I later found out that the bear was being transported from Gerald Durrell's Zoo in Jersey to Norwich Zoo. What annoyed me was that Channel Airways must have known about the transport arrangement well in advance, and should have advised me so that I could give immediate clearance… Obviously, bears do not turn up at the airport at the last minute hoping that there is a spare seat available in the next aircraft!

In 1974 I was promoted to Senior Executive Officer, which meant I had to make another move. My promotion meant that my time in the Outdoor Service of the department was finished; I was appointed to the Accountant and Comptroller General Administration, located in the Southend-on-Sea headquarters. I was now in management and in charge of three branches of the A&CO's office, with around 50 staff. In addition to staffing issues, I was also required to be involved in Policy and Systems matters. Quite a contrast to my previous 26 years' activities! As regards staff management, I was determined not to be just a figurehead, but to involve myself with the work requirements of each member of my staff. I had an open-door policy and wanted them to know that they could approach me whenever they had any concerns or problems.

Fortunately for me, the branch heads were first class. Two of them, like me, had also served in the Outdoor Service. One branch dealt with revenue statistics, which included the weekly compilation of the UK's resources account, payable to the European Union. This was the total of all VAT and import duty receipts on a weekly basis. The other two branches dealt with all matters arising from the aggregate of all the accounts from every C&E collection. In particular was the provision of the monthly computer tape for the collection of all deferred duty payments. This was another EU requirement which, in theory, allowed importers 30 days before paying the duty due from each importation. In practice, all such amounts due in a calendar month were totalled for payment by direct debit on the 15th of the following month, so it was vital that all the individual accounts were double-checked to ensure that the debits were correct.

In 1977 the department formed an Internal Audit Unit. This interested me, so I applied to join it. I was accepted, and became a founder member. I spent five years in the Internal Audit Unit before I retired in 1982. Part of the unit was located in London, and the other part in Southend. Luckily I was assigned to the latter. It was not audit work in the traditional accounting sense, but systems audit, operated by small teams. I was a team leader with three other auditors. It was demanding in that when a project was started, it involved a lot of research before the system was tested to check for weaknesses and to make improvements.

For example, I had one very successful financial outcome for the department, which is worth recording. From time to time, I would receive visits from members of the EU Court of Auditors. On this occasion the visiting auditor wished to check whether a recently introduced import entry system was working satisfactorily. It allowed a trader who regularly had large imports to dispense, to bypass conventional entry documentation on each occasion, provided he had a computer system and could submit comprehensive print-outs recording each transaction to the local excise office at the end of each month. At the same time, he had to record the total monthly duty to be paid and send it to our computer department. Self-assessment, we would call it now.

However, in the late 1970s the system was very new and computers were in their infancy, used mainly by commercial or industrial organisations. I had to make regular visits to traders using the system and one day went to see a computer manufacturer, anticipating that everything would be in order because he knew about computers. How wrong could I be!

Whenever I was making any kind of enquiry, I would try to obtain as much relevant information about the subject beforehand. I obtained a print-out showing the monthly duty payments so far that year up to the time of our visit in November. It showed that for the first four months, the monthly duty payment was in the region of £120,000. After that, each month it became less, ending up around £70,000, for no apparent reason. When I visited the trader and raised the matter with the Accounts department, they said they'd noticed the decrease, but couldn't explain it, as there had been no change in the scale of manufacture. I was not satisfied because there had to be a reason for it. But, how to proceed?

I decided to borrow the previous monthly printouts from the excise office which were very extensive. That evening, after dinner in my hotel, I started to examine them. Nothing came to light so far as the first few pages were concerned, and I was beginning to think I was wasting my time when I noticed that the duty calculation on one line was less than it should have been. Subsequent pages revealed similar discrepancies.

On my return to Southend, we referred the matter to our computer bureau to investigate. What transpired was not fraud, but a result of genuine computer error. Most programmes included a fail-safe check, but this trader had added a further check to his system which turned out to be faulty and had made the programme go berserk! The final result was that we received an adjusting duty payment of near £400,000.

As retirement loomed, the Chief Internal Auditor said

he would like me to stay for another 3 years. I politely declined, as I had always intended to retire at 60 years old. I have now been retired for 35 years, and if I live for another 4 years, I will have collected my pension for as long as I worked!

Postscript

2000-2006

This final chapter tells the story of how a phone call out of the blue led to my revisiting Hamilton and Mount Hope in Ontario, Canada. I will always be grateful for the pleasure and happiness I've gained from new friendships and experiences at this stage of my life.

The unexpected sequence of events started, as I've said, when the phone rang one evening in the millennium year 2000.

"You won't know who I am," chirps the voice, "but I'm ringing from *The Daily Mail*. I work for a section called 'Missing and Found', which comes out every Saturday. And I'm calling to ask you if you know a Charles Harte."

"Certainly do! Why?"

"He's been trying to locate you after all these years. Said you'd lost contact after the war. He knew you originally came from Camberley, Surrey, and that your wife's name was Betty. He sent me a photo of the two of you in Jack Dempsey's bar in New York!"

"Wow!"

"I'm so glad we've tracked you down. Have you any objection to me putting you both in touch?"

"None at all! I'd be delighted."

Five minutes later, my mate, Charlie, erstwhile drinking partner across the pond, called me and we had a long catch-up. We agreed to talk some more and to meet up soon.

If *The Mail* is successful in reuniting people, they print the outcome. So later that year, I was doing the crossword and my eyes fell on the picture of Charlie and me, not in New York, as Charlie had thought, but in New Canaan, Connecticut, at the home of John Hersam, a local newspaper owner. We were guests there one Sunday when visiting nearby Stamford. Our published names and details had, amazingly, already led to more people getting in touch with the paper, including a lady from Poole who needed help with some research. When visiting relatives in Hamilton, Ontario, the previous year, she'd been to a church close to the airfield where we'd trained, and had found the graves of fourteen RAF men, twelve of whom had died in three separate flying accidents at Mount Hope. Someone on the church council had asked her, as she was English, if she'd be interested in writing a history of the airmen buried in the churchyard. She'd seen the article about Charlie and me and got in touch.

Neither of us could help directly as there'd been no fatal flying accidents at the time we'd been at Hamilton, but I offered to contact a local friend of mine, Derek Rowe, who might know more and who had a huge archive of wartime memorabilia. Derek and I were both members of the Southend branch of the RAF Association (RAFA) and one evening, chatting over our WW2 careers, we'd discovered that we'd both been stationed at Mount Hope.

Derek, as a Staff Pilot, had flown on training flights after I'd been through training and he was still in touch with various members of the permanent staff. Upstairs in his house in Leigh-on-Sea – which he'd affectionately named *Mount Hope* – he had amassed an incredible collection of documentation from the war. Indeed, he found a copy of the actual letter the CO at Mount Hope had written to the parents of one of the airmen killed. He was also able to provide some photos of the interment ceremony with a lone bugler playing the last post.

Our Dorset researcher, on her visit to Canada, had attended a moving service to honour the fourteen airmen who'd lost their lives. We found out from her that this Decoration Service, as it was called, had been started after the war and was held every September to remember the dead.

Derek and I decided we would go to it the following year.

* * *

So in 2002 we returned to Canada.

The minister of the church had been informed, ahead of our visit, that we were coming to attend the Decoration Service and we received a letter of welcome from Joyce Timson, a member of the church, who, along with her husband, lovingly looked after the airmen's graves. Joyce and Bob were to become our main friends during our subsequent trips to Canada, but I'm getting ahead of myself.

On the flight over with *Air Canada* we got talking to one of the air stewardesses who spotted our blazer badges and asked us why we were visiting her country. When we explained, she told us that, as ex-aircrew, we would normally have been invited along to the cockpit, but this was no longer possible after the 9/11 attacks. However, they would be delighted if we could go along and meet the pilot after the plane had landed, which we duly did. We were also presented with a bottle of champagne each as a gift from the crew. What a welcome!

The Decoration Service was very moving. After the regular Sunday morning service, everyone goes outside to the graveyard and flowers are put on the graves, red white and blue bouquets. There are prayers and, as each airman's name is called, a member of the Black Knight Squadron, Royal Canadian Air Cadets, stands in front of the grave, salutes and places the flowers. Such is the local respect for all the RAF members who were at Mount Hope that an RAF Remembrance Garden has been created at the side of the church, overlooking the graveyard.

We met so many people during our visit and the hospitality was incredible. As we'd trained at Hamilton during the war, we were welcomed into the community and made to feel that we belonged. Time and time again we tried to repay everyone for their hospitality, by buying drinks or meals, but we were never allowed to.

Among many people who came forward to introduce themselves was an ex-RAF Scot, Frank Boyd, who had also been a staff pilot at Mount Hope and, soon after the end of the war, had emigrated to Canada. In my log book, I had a training flight detail with names on it and discovered that he and I had both been in the ops room at the same time on a night in 1943.

During the visit we were also taken to the Canadian Heritage Warplane Museum, near the International airport, where we went on a flight in a Dakota, which brought back many memories.

And finally, towards the end of our stay in Canada, I left Derek with the Timsons while I flew to Ottawa for a poignant meeting with my pilot, Court, from 107 Squadron, and his wife, Helen. Though we'd met up since the war, this was the first time I'd been to see them at home in Canada. We all went to visit Eric Smith, another Canadian pilot, who had served with us on 107. Eric had had the distinction of being the first one on the squadron to shoot down a V-1 before it reached its target. This buzz bomb rocket or *doodlebug*, as it was known, was an early cruise missile,

Dakota KN546, from the Canadian Warplane Heritage Museum, in flight above the Annapolis Valley, Nova Scotia.

developed by the *Luftwaffe* and aimed at specific locations in south-east England.

* * *

We decided to return to Hamilton again the following year, in 2003, when the highlight of our visit was a dinner in our honour at St Paul's Anglican Church Hall, the night after our arrival. There were many familiar faces there and we couldn't believe that the occasion had been organised just for our visit.

By a strange coincidence, we met up with Frank Boyd again when Bob and Joyce took us to Port Dover, on the shores of Lake Erie, for the day. Frank was dining at the same restaurant there. The sad part of the story came when he told us that he visited Port Dover regularly because his son had been killed and was buried there. He has now become one of the friends, along with the Timsons, we meet each time we go.

As you'll have gathered, we were to return to Canada again… and again. Five times in all: in 2002, 2003, 2005, 2007 and 2010.

In 2005, when my partner, Pam Blackaby, came to Canada with us, Derek and I received letters from the Hamilton City Authority asking if we would unveil a special plaque to commemorate the fourteen airmen, directly after the annual Decoration Service. The graves had by now been officially listed, along with many others, by the War Graves Commission.

At the unveiling of the plaque, as well as the cadets

there were also veterans, the local and provincial MPs, and members of the Royal Canadian Airforce Association, amongst those who attended this commemoration of men who paid the ultimate sacrifice and died far from home.

What had started out as one visit for Derek and me, has led, through a very large snowball effect, to meetings with more and more people, all linked by a place and a time, in one way or another. Even the man whose grandfather had owned the land which government requisitioned for the airfield! I've now got to know many of the Royal Canadian Airforce Association, 447 Wing, the Canadian chapter of the RAF regiment, as well as the group of friends I made on the first visits. Shared history is a powerful way of bringing people together and keeping them in touch.

I wanted to see the Gilliatts again so, on this visit, Pam and I flew from Hamilton to Ottawa, where Court and Helen had moved into a retirement centre at Kanata, just outside the city. When I phoned Helen to arrange accommodation, she insisted on putting us up at their expense. Imagine our surprise when we found we were booked into a lovely top floor room, at the Best Western in Ottawa, with amazing views of the Houses of Parliament.

Every time we went back to Canada we thought it couldn't possibly be as good as the previous visits... but it always was! It got better and better. On our last visit in 2010, after the Decoration Service we all adjourned to the new HQ of 447 Wing, of the RCA Association. The president, Bill Grahlman came over and asked Derek and me if we would lay a wreath on behalf of the RAF at the Hamilton war memorial the following weekend for Battle of Britain

Sunday. What an honour! The parade was amazing – with so many civilians attending. The Canadians are fervently patriotic and so respectful of those who died in the wars. At the dinner afterwards, Derek and I were given a special mention in the speeches.

In one room of HQ I was shown a large scale model of an Anson aircraft and introduced to the person who made it. Would you believe it… when I checked my logbook I found I had actually flown in the same plane with the same identification markings as part of a training flight exercise.

Another highlight of the 2010 trip happened soon after our arrival at the Crown Plaza Hotel where we'd stayed on our previous two visits. Our favourite barmaid, Debbie, rushed over as we entered the restaurant: "Not you two again!" she exclaimed, giving us hugs and kisses. "It's a whisky and soda and a gin and tonic. Right?"

What a memory! It was three years since we'd been there. Cynics might say that we must have frequented the bar quite a few times during our visits, but it was still impressive. "By the way," she added, "they're on the house, along with dinner tonight!"

Another evening at dinner, the hotel's managing director rang through to the bar and asked whether he could join us the following morning for breakfast as he was very keen on the history of the RAF and aviation, and wanted to meet us. Of course we agreed. Oh, and by the way, dinner and drinks were on the house again! (Would this generosity be extended in the UK, I wondered.)

* * *

and FOUND!

CHARLES HARTE of Rotherham, South Yorkshire, and **John Hill** of Leigh-on-Sea, Essex, are now septuagenarian grandfathers.

But during World War II they were RAF navigators flying on bombing raids over Germany.

And they're back together again, after a 55-year gap.

Charles and John met while training at an RAF base in Torquay in 1942. They then spent a year with a unit in Canada. 'We had great times at the Royal Canadian Air Force base near Hamilton, Ontario,' says Charles.

But on their return to Britain in 1944, they were posted to different places and lost touch.

Charles served with 487 Squadron near Southampton. He went on 25 night raids, through heavy flak, but his plane was never hit.

'We flew a Mosquito,' he says, 'a twin-engined fighter-bomber — a marvellous machine. I came home from the war unscathed, as did Johnny.' Two very lucky men.

After the war, John worked

Reunited: RAF colleagues John Hill, left, and Charles Harte in 1944

as a HM Customs and Excise official, while Charles was a sales rep for various companies.

Charles, a widower, has suffered from strokes during the past year, so he hasn't yet been able to visit John.

But, with that old wartime fighting spirit, he is determined to get better and make the trip in the New Year.

■ *IF THERE is someone you would like to trace, write to Gill Whitley, 88 Tan-yr-efail, Holyhead, Anglesey LL65 2SD, enclosing SAE, or send an e-mail to monica.porter@dailymail.co.uk — including a contact phone number. All communications will be answered as soon as possible. This column is researched with the aid of UK Info-Disc, sales: 08000 192 192.*

WE DID WHAT WE HAD TO

In an earlier chapter I mentioned that Court, my pilot, was no longer with us. In 2007 I took advantage of the good flight links between Hamilton and Ottawa, which meant I could take the first flight out in the morning and return the same day on the last flight back. I spent the day with Court and Helen, which included lunch out at a local restaurant. I'm so glad I made the effort because it turned out to be the last time I saw Court. He died the following year.

I also have to report that Derek died last August, 2015. I've been told that he was fondly remembered at the Decoration Service this year.

Although we kept in touch, I regret that, sadly, Charlie Harte and I were never to meet up. I was no longer driving long distances and Charlie suffered a severe stroke, affecting his mobility. He died five years ago.

* * *

I think, by now, you'll have gathered that I have an incredible fondness for Canada and for all the people I've met. Derek and I both agreed, on many occasions, that in our respective RAF careers, the best posting for both of us was to Mount Hope. I want to put on record my gratitude for all the generous hospitality I've received on each and every visit, for whisky and sodas and so much else, and for the genuine friendships I've made. I still talk regularly to Joyce on the phone and my Xmas card list has grown and grown, instead of shrinking.

I would love to go back to Canada one more time.

Finally I must also record what I feel is a fitting end

to this narrative. As members of the Canadian Warplane Heritage Museum at Mount Hope we always paid it a visit each time we were in Hamilton. Among their collection of WW2 vintage aircraft is the only other airworthy Lancaster. In 2014 arrangements were made for this plane to leave Canada for the first time and fly to the UK where it could join its fellow in the Battle of Britain Memorial Flight, as well as participating in air displays that year. In the south of England there were several two-day events in which the Lancasters were to make an overnight stop at Biggin Hill, rather than go all the way back to the Memorial Base in Lincolnshire. However, strong cross winds made this risky, so to my delight they came to my local airport at Southend. One Friday afternoon in late August, I was working down the end of my garden when I heard the unmistakable sound of Merlin engines. I looked up and saw the two Lancasters flying quite low in close formation over the rooftop of my house, directly towards me. As far as I was concerned, it was my own personal flypast!

Per ardua ad astra.

* * *

P.P.S. At the end of August 2016 I was interviewed and filmed by a representative of the De Havilland Air Museum for a film they were making, as part of the *Mosquito Veterans Project*. This led to an article about me and my wartime RAF career in my local paper, *The Leigh Times*.

My 2005 visit to Canada

HISTORICAL HAPPENINGS

Plaque honours RAF veterans

BY ART FRENCH
The Glanbrook Gazette

"They slipped the surly bonds of earth." Paraphrasing John McGee's poem "High Flight", this is the heading on the newest historical plaque in Glanbrook, unveiled last Sunday at St. Paul's Glanford Anglican church, Mount Hope. The special guests who did the official unveiling were three visitors from England.

John Hill and Derek Rowe were RAF members who served at Mount Hope in the later stages of WWII; Isobel Wilson, Dorset, England, is an avid historian who has researched and contacted the relatives of the 14 airmen buried at St. Paul's.

The day's programme began with a standing-room-only church service conducted by Reverend Patricia Lucy, her second week as the new minister at St. Paul's. Ceremonies, hosted by Glanbrook Heritage Society, were transferred outside for the unveiling of the RAF commemorative plaque.

The plaque was one approved by the Joint Plaquing Sub-committee of the Hamilton Historical board and Hamilton LACAC and financed by the City of Hamilton The activities finished with laying of flowers by members of 779 Air Cadet squadron and tributes by 447

Derek Rowe, left, RAF (ret.), Reverend Patricia Lucy, John Hill, RAF (ret.) participated in an nveiling of a commemorative plaque honouring the RAF men buried at St. Paul's Church in Mount Hope.

Art French/Gazette photo

Wing, RCAFA, Mount Hope. Divine intervention was declared as the threatening rain clouds stayed away and a single-engine Boeing Stearman from the Canadian Warplane Heritage museum flew overhead during a minute of silence in the closing moments of the ceremony.

Navy blazers, brilliant red poppies and glistening medals were prominent among the gathered assembly to honour those who died away from home but will always be remembered, near and far.

To finish the day, quoting Reverend Lucy, "In the spirit of true Anglicanism, refreshments are being served in the parish hall."

"At the going down of the sun and in the morning
We will remember them."
From "The Fallen", a poem by Laurence Binyon, 1914.

93

RAF Garden of Remembrance at St Paul's Anglican Church, Mount Hope, Hamilton, Ontario, Canada, 2005.

From the citizens of Hamilton,
in tribute to those sterling qualities
which prompted you to accept
the hazards of war,
in order that, by the grace of God,
a grateful country may continue to
live in peace and security.

Inscription on Medal :
The people of Hamilton Remember Your Victory Our Freedom

Canada revisited yet again

Towards the end of September, accompanied by Pam Blackaby and, as previously by my local R.A.F.A. friend, Derek Rowe, I set off on a two week visit to Hamilton, Ontario. As with the visits Derek and I made in 2002 and 2003 this was planned to coincide with the annual R.A.F. Decoration Service held at St. Paul's Anglican Church, Mount Hope near the airfield where we were both stationed in 1943/4. It was very fortuitous since this year's visit coincided with the erection of a plaque, in the church R.A.F. Garden of Remembrance, which commemorates the British Air Training Plan during World War II and the 16 R.A.F. servicemen who died whilst serving at Mount Hope, 14 of whom are buried at St. Paul's.

A short while before our departure, Derek and I received a letter from the City Hall Administration, Hamilton , inviting us to perform the unveiling of the plaque. The writing on the plaque is displayed on the accompanying photograph. And the heading "They slipped the surly bonds of earth" is a paraphrase of the first line of John McGee's poem "High Flight". John McGee was an American who enlisted in the Royal Canadian Air Force and was stationed at Digby in Lincolnshire when he wrote his poem in September 1941 (He was killed three months later, aged just 19, when his aircraft collided with one flying from nearby Cranwell.)

After the ceremony we were presented with a "1945 -2005 Hamilton Remembers Certificate of Appreciation" signed by the Mayor, and a commemorative medal. This was an altogether unforgettable experience.

Another highlights of our visit was an invitation to a Corn Roast Party at a local farm where freshly picked corn on the cob were boiled in a metal container over an open wood fire and then dipped in a vat of floating hot melted butter.

A few days later we journeyed to Toronto where we were invited to lunch at the prestigious Royal Canadian Military Institute by a member, a friend of Derek's, who emigrated to Toronto from Leigh on Sea many years ago.

Pam and I spent the final weekend in Ottawa where I was pleased to meet up again with my war-time Canadian pilot and his wife. On the Sunday the four of us were joined for lunch by another contemporary Canadian ex-pilot and his wife. Plenty of reminiscing ensued and Pam felt honoured to be in the company of these two men who while serving with my squadron were both awarded a Distinguished Flying Cross.

The hospitality and generosity we received from all our Canadian friends was fantastic. I could not help noticing that nearly all public buildings and several private dwellings were flying the Canadian flag daily. If only we were similarly outgoing in Britain!

John Hill

John served as a navigator in Mosquitos. He received his training at the Mount. Hope, Hamilton Canada air base. He went on to fly 46 operational missions during the war. His friend, Derek Rowe was a mosquito pilot who also did his training at Mount Hope.

John has attended several of these Annual R.A.F. Decoration Services organised by the Anglican Church at Mount Hope where the 16 service men who died while they were training there are commemorated.

Ed.

My article in The Fairway magazine, November 2005

Photos from my visit to Canada, 2010.

Branch 163 Mount Hamilton Royal Canadian Legion

With

447 Wing Royal Canadian
Air Force Association

COMMEMORATES THE
70TH ANNIVERSARY

OF

THE BATTLE OF BRITAIN

1940 – 2010

Sunday September 19, 2010

Branch 163 Memorial Garden
435 Limeridge Road East.
Hamilton, Ontario

Lightning Source UK Ltd.
Milton Keynes UK
UKHW022045251122
412793UK00014B/1047